T0323280

Mastering the Job Market

THE SIOP PROFESSIONAL PRACTICE SERIES

Series Editor
Nancy T. Tippins

Titles in the Series

Performance Management Transformation: Lessons Learned and Next Steps
Edited by Elaine D. Pulakos and Mariangela Battista

Employee Surveys and Sensing: Challenges and Opportunities
Edited by William H. Macey and Alexis A. Fink

Mastering Industrial-Organizational Psychology: Training Issues
for Master's Level I-O Psychologists
Edited by Elizabeth L. Shoenfelt

Mastering the Job Market

Career Issues for Master's Level
Industrial-Organizational Psychologists

Edited by

ELIZABETH L. SHOENFELT

Published in partnership with

OXFORD
UNIVERSITY PRESS

OXFORD
UNIVERSITY PRESS

Oxford University Press is a department of the University of Oxford. It furthers
the University's objective of excellence in research, scholarship, and education
by publishing worldwide. Oxford is a registered trade mark of Oxford University
Press in the UK and certain other countries.

Published in the United States of America by Oxford University Press
198 Madison Avenue, New York, NY 10016, United States of America.

Library of Congress Cataloging-in-Publication Data
Names: Shoenfelt, Elizabeth L., editor.
Title: Mastering the job market : career issues for master's level
industrial-organizational psychologists / edited by Elizabeth L. Shoenfelt.
Description: New York, NY : Oxford University Press, [2021] |
Series: Society industrial organizational psych |
Includes bibliographical references and index.
Identifiers: LCCN 2020025130 (print) | LCCN 2020025131 (ebook) |
ISBN 9780190071172 (hardback) | ISBN 9780190071196 (epub) |
ISBN 9780197549223
Subjects: LCSH: Psychology, Industrial—Vocational guidance. |
Industrial Psychologists—Training of.
Classification: LCC HF5548.8 .M3744 2021 (print) | LCC HF5548.8 (ebook) |
DDC 158.7023—dc23
LC record available at https://lccn.loc.gov/2020025130
LC ebook record available at https://lccn.loc.gov/2020025131

DOI: 10.1093/oso/9780190071172.001.0001

1 3 5 7 9 8 6 4 2

Printed by Integrated Books International, United States of America

Contents

Preface

I was honored when the Professional Practice Series Committee of the Society for Industrial and Organizational Psychology (SIOP) invited me to propose and then edit this book, *Mastering the Job Market: Career Issues for Master's Level Industrial-Organizational Psychologists*, and its sister volume, *Mastering Industrial-Organizational Psychology: Training Issues for Master's Level I-O Psychologists*, both focusing on master's-level industrial-organizational (I-O) issues. The field of I-O psychology has been spotlighted recently by the U.S. Bureau of Labor Statistics as one of the fastest-growing occupations in the nation (ABC News, 2014) and continues to be recognized as a top job (Bureau of Labor Statistics, 2019). The American Psychological Association has taken note of the growth in I-O master's programs and the success of I-O master's graduates in the job market (Bailey, 2020). The strong job market for I-O psychologists is predicted to remain so for at least the next decade (Bureau of Labor Statistics, 2018).

Master's graduate training programs in I-O psychology have exponentially increased in number over the past several decades, from fewer than 20 in the early 1980s to more than 170 master's programs currently listed on the SIOP website (SIOP, 2019). I-O master's programs now outnumber doctoral programs and produce a larger number of graduates. Master's programs and master's graduates outnumber their doctoral-level counterparts. Estimates based on the SIOP website suggest more than three times as many graduate each year from master's programs (1,850) as from doctoral programs (520; Shoenfelt, Stone, & Kottke, 2018). Concomitantly with the growth in master's programs, SIOP has devoted more resources and attention to master's issues, as evidenced by these two books in the SIOP Professional Practice Series. When I contacted I-O master's program directors and faculty to serve as authors of the books, they shared my excitement and enthusiasm for the books focused on I-O master's training and careers. This, the second book, provides data-based insight for I-O master's careers as well as practical guidance based on the experience and tacit knowledge of faculty and program directors from some of the top I-O master's programs in the nation.

Purpose and Audience

Mastering the Job Market: Career Issues for Master's Level Industrial-Organizational Psychologists targets two audiences. First, the book will provide valuable guidance to early career I-O practitioners, I-O master's graduate students, and faculty in I-O master's programs. Our book provides empirically based insight and guidance for all phases of an I-O practitioner's career, from initiating a job search and the application process to landing the first job to transitioning to new jobs/roles, as well as continuing education and development during the career. This book is particularly appropriate for a graduate course on professional and career issues.

Our second audience comprises psychology faculty members and undergraduates interested in careers as I-O practitioners. SIOP members lament that I-O psychology is not well known to those outside the discipline (e.g., Ryan, 2003), even by other psychologists (Gasser, Whitsett, Mosley, Sullivan, Rogers, & Tan, 1998). Accordingly, many psychology faculty are unaware of careers in I-O psychology as they advise promising undergraduates. This volume will assist with advising undergraduates and will inform advisors about careers as I-O master's-level practitioners, hopefully bringing interested students into the field of I-O psychology. Our book will provide prospective students with information on jobs and careers available to I-O master's graduates, including essential competencies and experiences for career success, and how to apply for jobs.

Overview of the Volume

Mastering the Job Market: Career Issues for Master's Level Industrial-Organizational Psychologists begins with an introduction to the field of I-O psychology and presents the empirical basis for the book, a large-scale survey of I-O master's graduates and a second survey of their employers. Survey methodology and demographic data for I-O master's graduates and employers are presented. The remaining six chapters of this volume address a myriad of issues related to the careers of master's-level I-O psychologists based on the survey data and insights from I-O master's faculty from top-ranked I-O master's programs.

In Chapter 2, L'Heureux and Van Hein provide information about job opportunities available to I-O master's graduates. The authors draw heavily on the Graduate Survey data to identify common occupational titles, organizational roles, and salary ranges for both recent I-O graduates and those later in their careers. Job positions reflect a broad range of roles that include talent management, data analytics, human resources, organization development, and consulting. I-O psychology master's graduates overwhelmingly perceive their I-O degree to be valuable and report a high level of career satisfaction.

In Chapter 3, Glazer, Moon, Ayman, and Berger take a deep dive into the Graduate Survey and Employer Survey data to identify essential competencies for success as an I-O practitioner. In addition to core I-O knowledge and skills, enabling competencies such as oral communication, business acumen and consulting skills, and project management are key. Ethics and business/technical writing likewise were highly rated by both I-O master's graduates and employers. Top competencies identified by work sector were job analysis (government), data analysis (education), project management (nonprofit), and consulting skills (private sector and consulting).

Walker, Bartels, and Shahani-Denning provide an abundance of advice in Chapter 4 for the job search and offer specific strategies and actions. Actions in graduate school that lay a foundation for a successful job search include developing an elevator speech, pursuing internships (paid or unpaid), participating in applied projects, and ensuring a professional social media image. The authors provide strategies for completing an application, using applicant tracking systems, writing résumés and cover letters, responding to phone screens, preparing for interviews, and demonstrating job offer etiquette. These critical insights into the nuts and bolts of conducting a job search help to ensure success.

Cunningham and Reilly provide advice on the lifelong journey of one's career in Chapter 5 using the metaphor of the many stops on a train ride to discuss on-boarding and off-boarding processes. Cunningham and Reilly explore the realities of major career transitions starting with graduate students who become master's-degree holders with a first real job and then make the transition from one position, role, or organization to another as their careers develop. The authors examine formal and informal on-boarding and off-boarding procedures for master's-level I-O psychology practitioners and provide insight into how to successfully pursue career objectives and manage challenging career transitions.

In Chapter 6, Mazzola, Chrobot-Mason, and Cox address the important postgraduate experience of continuing training and development for I-O master's graduates. The authors discuss common certifications and continuing education opportunities relevant to the careers of I-O master's practitioners. Graduate Survey data are used to describe mentoring experienced by I-O master's graduates and their employers. Three best-practice suggestions for maximizing mentoring relationships are offered. The authors recommend that I-O master's practitioners use mentoring and professional development opportunities to facilitate their career advancement.

In the final chapter of this book, Chapter 7, Nagy, Aziz, and Schroeder discuss the professional identity of I-O master's graduates. Implications for licensure within I-O psychology are reviewed, and the authors make an important distinction between licensing and certification/credentialing. They argue that establishing an I-O psychology certification process may be a viable means to maintain an identity or brand while encouraging consistent graduate training in the field of I-O psychology. Graduate Survey results are presented to highlight the benefits of professional membership. The authors provide suggestions for developing the professional identity of master's I-O psychology graduates in the future.

Of note, the SIOP Professional Practice Series sister volume to this book, *Mastering Industrial-Organizational Psychology: Training Issues for Master's Level I-O Psychologists* (Shoenfelt, 2020), provides best practices for training master's-level I-O psychologists offered by faculty from top-ranked I-O master's programs (Acikgoz et al., 2018; Vodanovich, Morganson, & Kass, 2018).

It is my hope that *Mastering the Job Market: Career Issues for Master's Level Industrial-Organizational Psychologists* proves interesting, informative, and useful for all readers curious about the careers of I-O master's-level psychologists.

Betsy Shoenfelt

References

ABC News. (2014). https://abcnews.go.com/Business/americas-20-fastest-growing-jobs-surprise/story?id=22364716

Acikgoz, Y., Huelsman, T. J., Swets J. L., Dixon, A. R., Jeffer, S. N., Olsen, D. R., & Rosset, A. (2018). The cream of the crop: Student and alumni perceptions of I-O psychology master's degree program quality. *The Industrial-Organizational Psychologist*, 55(4). http://my.siop.org/tip/jan18/editor/ArtMID/13745/ArticleID/334/The-Cream-of-the-Crop-Student-and-Alumni-Perceptions-of-I-O-Psychology-Masters-Degree-Program-Quality

Bailey, D. (2020, January/February). Special report: Top 10 trends for 2020. *Monitor on Psychology: A Publication of the American Psychological Association, 51*(1), 38–75.

Bureau of Labor Statistics. (2018, May). https://www.bls.gov/oes/current/oes193032.htm

Bureau of Labor Statistics. (2019). Occupational employment statistics. https://www.bls.gov/oes/current/oes193032.htm

Gasser, M., Whitsett, D., Mosley, N., Sullivan, K., Rogers, T., & Tan, R. (1998). I-O psychology: What's your line? *The Industrial-Organizational Psychologist, 35*(4). https://doi.org/10.1037/e577062011-013

Ryan, A. M. (2003). Defining ourselves: I-O psychology's identity quest. *The Industrial-Organizational Psychologist, 41*(1), 21–33. https://doi.org/10.1037/e578792011-002

Shoenfelt, E. L. (Ed.) (2020). *Mastering industrial-organizational psychology: Training issues for master's level I-O psychologists.* New York: Oxford University Press.

Shoenfelt, E. L., Stone, N. J., & Kottke, J. L. (2018). Gaining organizational entry and developing partnerships for applied research and experience: A perspective from industrial-organizational psychology master's programs. *Industrial and Organizational Psychology: Perspectives on Science and Practice, 11*, 606–612.

Society for Industrial and Organizational Psychology, Inc. (2016). *Guidelines for education and training in industrial-organizational psychology.* Bowling Green, OH: Author. https://www.siop.org/Events-Education/Graduate-Training-Program/Guidelines-for-Education-and-Training

Society for Industrial and Organizational Psychology, Inc. (2019). http://siop.org/GTP/

Vodanovich, S. J., Morganson, V. J., & Kass, S. J. (2018). Ranking I-O master's programs using objective data from I-O coordinators. *The Industrial-Organizational Psychologist, 55*(4). http://my.siop.org/tip/jan18/editor/ArtMID/13745/ArticleID/333/Ranking-I-O-Masters-Programs-Using-Objective-Data-From-I-O-Coordinators1

Author Biographies

Roya Ayman is a Professor of I-O Psychology in the Department of Psychology, Illinois Institute of Technology. She was the director of the I-O program from 1989 to 2019 and is the advisor for her students, as well as for Erasmus+ program exchange students from Valencia, Spain. She has been a visiting professor at the Human Resource Management Department of the National Institute of Development Advancement in Bangkok, Thailand, since 2011. Dr. Ayman is an SIOP Fellow, is a Fellow from the Leadership Trust Foundation, Herefordshire, UK, and received the Dean's leadership award. She has co-edited two books, each touching on her main areas of research: leadership and work–family interface considering gender and cultural impact. She is on the editorial boards of *Leadership Quarterly, Journal of Business and Psychology, Group and Organizational Management*, and *International Journal of Cross-Cultural Management*. Finally, Dr. Ayman served on executive and advisory boards of nonprofit organizations and conducts training.

Shahnaz Aziz is an Associate Professor and Industrial/Organizational Psychology Program Director at East Carolina University (ECU). She earned her PhD from Bowling Green State University. Shahnaz is a well-published researcher and has presented at numerous conferences. She mainly conducts studies in the areas of workaholism and work–life balance. Currently, Shahnaz's lab is involved in investigating the influence of workaholism on employee health and well-being. She was a co-investigator on a multidisciplinary research grant funded by the National Science Foundation. Additionally, Shahnaz was a recipient of the following awards: UNC Board of Governors Distinguished Professor for Teaching Award; ECU Psychology Department Faculty Appreciation Award for Graduate Student Mentoring; and ECU Arts & Sciences Summer Research Award. She was a finalist for ECU's Distinguished Graduate Mentoring Award. Finally, Shahnaz is a member of ECU's Graduate Council and SIOP's Membership Committee and was Vice-Chair of North Carolina Industrial/Organizational Psychologists executive committee.

Lynn K. Bartels is a Professor of Industrial-Organizational Psychology at Southern Illinois University Edwardsville (SIUE). In addition to her role as a faculty member, she serves as the Director of Faculty Development for SIUE. She teaches courses in Personnel Psychology, Employee Development, and Employee Selection. Her research interests include employee discrimination in all forms, particularly weight discrimination. She works in the areas of assessment centers and employment interviews. She is currently working on a project to recruit, retain, and promote female faculty in STEM and an initiative to increase the use of flipped teaching in STEM courses. She earned her doctorate from the University of Akron in 1991.

Rita Berger is an associate professor in the Department of Social and Quantitative Psychology of the Universitat de Barcelona, where she teaches courses in organizational and work psychology, and research. After earning her doctoral degree in psychology at the Ludwig-Maximilians Universität Munich (Germany), Dr. Berger has worked on numerous research projects granted by the European Commission on topics like health at work, excellence, leadership, and teams at cross-cultural levels. She has published several articles on leadership and teams. She is a member of the European Association of Work and Organizational Psychology (EAWOP).

Donna Chrobot-Mason is as an Associate Professor and Director of the Center for Organizational Leadership at the University of Cincinnati. Her research focuses on leadership across differences and strategies for creating organizational practices, policies, and climates that support diversity and foster intergroup collaboration. Donna holds a PhD and master's degree in applied psychology from the University of Georgia and teaches undergraduate and graduate courses in human resources, diversity, and organizational leadership. Donna has published articles in journals such as the *Journal of Management, Leadership Quarterly, International Journal of Human Resource Management, Journal of Organizational Behavior,* and *Group and Organization Management.* She has served on the editorial review board for the *Journal of Management, Personnel Psychology,* and the *Journal of Business and Psychology.* Her book (co-authored with Chris Ernst), *Boundary Spanning Leadership: Six Practices for Solving Problems, Driving Innovation, and Transforming Organizations,* was published by McGraw-Hill Professional in 2010.

Cody B. Cox received his PhD from Rice University in 2010 and has taught undergraduate and graduate students in business schools and psychology programs. Dr. Cox teaches in Greehey Business School at St. Mary's

University in San Antonio, Texas. He teaches graduate and undergraduate courses on topics such as organizational psychology, human resource management, advanced statistics, and leadership. Dr. Cox joined St. Mary's University in 2016 after teaching at Texas A&M University San Antonio and the University of Texas at Brownsville. He teaches in the graduate Industrial-Organizational Psychology Program and the Greehey School of Business, where he is currently Chair of Management and Marketing. Since receiving his PhD, Dr. Cox has published 19 peer-reviewed papers and delivered 40 presentations at regional and national professional conferences. Dr. Cox won the National Society of Leadership and Success Excellence in Teaching Award in 2015 and the Greehey School of Business Research Award in 2018.

Christopher J. L. Cunningham is a UC Foundation Professor and Graduate Program Director of the Master's of Science degree program at the University of Tennessee at Chattanooga (UTC). He regularly teaches and conducts research in the areas of occupational health psychology, organizational psychology, organizational development, and quantitative/qualitative research and evaluation methods. Outside of UTC, Chris is active in a variety of consulting and service engagements, primarily as Chief Science Officer at Logi-Serve and as an Executive Committee member for the Society for Occupational Health Psychology. Chris earned a BA in Psychology at Lehigh University and a MA and PhD in I-O Psychology at Bowling Green State University. Chris has been linked to UTC's longstanding master's program since 2007 and sincerely appreciates his amazing colleagues, students, and program alumni.

Sharon Glazer is Professor and Chair of the Division of Applied Behavioral Sciences at the University of Baltimore and program director for the new Global I-O Psychology certificate. She serves as the local coordinator for the Erasmus+ Master's in Work, Organizational, and Personnel Psychology headquartered at the University of Valencia. After earning her PhD in I-O Psychology from Central Michigan University, Dr. Glazer completed a postdoctoral fellowship at the National Institute of Occupational Safety & Health. She was a visiting professor at universities in France, Spain, Portugal, Italy, and Hungary, and a research professor at the University of Maryland. Glazer served as treasurer for the International Association for Cross-Cultural Psychology, editor of the *International Journal of Stress Management*, and co-chair for the International Affairs Committee of SIOP. She is a Fellow of SIOP, the International Academy for Intercultural Research, and the International Association of Applied Psychology.

Tara J. L'Heureux has been a full-time faculty member in the Master's in Industrial-Organizational Psychology Program at the University of New Haven for over two decades. She received her PhD in industrial-organizational psychology from the University of Connecticut. An Assistant Professor in the Department of Psychology and Sociology at UNH, she teaches courses in organizational behavior, worker well-being, groups in organizations, industrial psychology, and statistics. Her research interests include the pedagogy of classroom teams, statistical literacy, and competency-based assessment of academic programs.

Joseph J. Mazzola is the Director of the Industrial-Organizational Psychology MA program and an Associate Professor at Meredith College. His research focuses on stress measurement and management, promoting healthy behaviors in the workplace such as proper nutrition and exercise habits, and the use of qualitative/mixed methodology. He has been published in several scholarly journals and books, including *Work & Stress*, *Journal of Occupational Health Psychology*, and *Stress & Health*. He is the current treasurer for the Society of Occupational Psychology and a member of the Society of Industrial-Organizational Psychology. Joe received his PhD in industrial-organizational psychology from the University of South Florida in 2010.

Simon M. Moon is an Associate Professor in the Department of Psychology at La Salle University, where he teaches courses in statistics, research methods, psychometrics, and I-O psychology. After earning his doctoral degree in I-O psychology at the University of Akron, Dr. Moon has worked on various research and grant projects that require the most up-to-date knowledge within the discipline and recently authored a textbook for the first-year graduate students. He is a member of the American Psychological Association's Division 5 (Division of Evaluation, Measurement, and Statistics) and Division 14.

Mark S. Nagy received his master's and doctoral degrees specializing in industrial-organizational psychology from Louisiana State University. He taught at Radford University for five years before becoming the Director of the Industrial-Organizational Psychology Master of Arts graduate program at Xavier University in 2000, and is still in that position. He has over 45 national conference presentations and 19 published articles in several journals, including *Industrial and Organizational Psychology: Perspectives on Science and Practice*, *The Industrial-Organizational Psychologist*, *Journal of*

Occupational and Organizational Psychology, and *Applied H.R.M. Research*. He has consulted for diverse organizations ranging from nonprofits to federal government agencies to for-profit private and public organizations. He has consulted on a variety of organizational projects, such as developing and analyzing employee assessments, conducting training needs assessments, providing statistical consultation, and creating and analyzing employee surveys. His current interests include civility in the workplace and employee engagement surveys.

Nora P. Reilly is a Professor and Coordinator of the master's program in I-O Psychology at Radford University. She earned her doctorate in social psychology from Dartmouth College and retrained in organizational psychology at Colorado State. More recently, her research interests have focused on ethical issues regarding quality of work life, though she continues to explore the regulation of emotions in the workplace as well as workplace stigma associated with veterans' transition to the civilian workforce. She has published in such outlets as *Academy of Management Journal, Motivation and Emotion, Journal of Vocational Behavior, Journal of Applied Social Psychology*, and *Journal of Business and Psychology*. Nora has taught more courses than she can recall, ranging from the bachelor's through the doctoral level, and enjoys a dedicated alumni network at Radford. In her spare time, she consults with organizations on leadership and assessment.

Daniel A. Schroeder is President/CEO of Organization Development Consultants, Inc. (ODC), a management consulting firm offering assessment-based performance solutions for individuals, teams, and organizations. ODC serves regional and national clients from its offices in suburban Milwaukee. Additionally, he teaches in the Organizational Behavior and Leadership (bachelor's) and Organization Development (master's) programs at Edgewood College (Madison, WI), programs that he founded and for which he served as Program Director. He earned his doctoral (Psychology/Organizational Science) and bachelor's (Psychology/Professional Business) degrees within the University of Wisconsin System. He earned his master's degree in Industrial-Organizational Psychology at Western Michigan University. He is a licensed psychologist in Wisconsin. He holds board certifications in organizational and business consulting psychology (OBCP) from the American Board of Professional Psychology and in psychology from the American Board of Psychological Specialties.

Comila Shahani-Denning is a Professor and Director of the Industrial-Organizational Master's Program at Hofstra University. Comila received her BA degree from St. Xavier's College and MA and PhD from Rice University. She teaches and supervises students in the Applied Organizational Psychology Doctoral Program. She teaches courses in research methods, industrial psychology, and personnel selection. She is currently involved in teaching the internship courses in both programs where she oversees student internships. Her research interests lie in the area of recruitment and selection, decision making, work–life balance, and leadership development.

Elizabeth L. Shoenfelt, University Distinguished Professor in the Department of Psychological Sciences at Western Kentucky University, has directed the WKU Industrial-Organizational Psychology Graduate Program for 25+ years. She received her PhD in 1983 from LSU in I-O Psychology with minors in Sport Psychology and Statistics. She is a licensed I-O Psychologist, a Certified Mental Performance Consultant® and Fellow of the Association for Applied Sport Psychology, and a member of the USOPC Sport Psychology and Mental Skills Registry. She is a Fellow in the Society for Industrial and Organizational Psychology (SIOP) and, in 2013, she received the SIOP Distinguished Teaching Contributions Award. She teaches graduate courses in I-O and directs thesis research and I-O internships. She has 35+ years of consulting experience in business, industry, government, education, and sports. Her I-O work focuses on selection, EEO issues, organizational justice in team settings, performance management, and pedagogical issues. In sports, she works with teams and individually with coaches and athletes at the intercollegiate, Olympic, and professional levels. In September 2020, Shoenfelt became the Senior Director for Applied Psychology with the American Psychological Association.

Judith L. Van Hein is a Professor of Psychology at Middle Tennessee State University (MTSU). She teaches employee selection, compensation, and general psychology. She received her PhD in industrial-organizational psychology from Georgia Institute of Technology. As a senior consultant with MTSU's Center for Organizational and Human Resource Effectiveness, she has worked with clients in various industries on projects regarding job analysis, employee surveys, training needs analysis, training, employee selection, promotion, and performance appraisal.

Susan A. Walker has over 30 years of experience working in the field of industrial-organizational psychology in both consulting and industry. Her

I-O consulting experience has included work with Psychological Services, Inc., American Institutes for Research for the Behavioral and Social Sciences, Army Research Institute, and Performance Associates. Her corporate work has included FedEx, FedEx Express, and FedEx Freight Corporation. Her responsibilities have included managing and hiring I-O psychologists and I-O psychology interns and leading employee selection, testing, employee survey, talent management, and leadership development programs. She earned her BA from Auburn University and a master's in I-O psychology from Western Kentucky University in 1990. Susan is on medical disability due to Parkinson's disease, which she has battled for over 20 years.

Contributors

Roya Ayman, PhD
Illinois Institute of Technology
Chicago, IL, USA

Shahnaz Aziz, PhD
East Carolina University
Greenville, NC, USA

Lynn K. Bartels, PhD
Southern Illinois University
Edwardsville
Edwardsville, IL, USA

Rita Berger, PhD
University of Barcelona
Barcelona, Spain

Donna Chrobot-Mason, PhD
University of Cincinnati
Cincinnati, OH, USA

Cody B. Cox, PhD
St. Mary's University
San Marcos, TX, USA

Christopher J. L. Cunningham, PhD
University of Tennessee at Chattanooga
Chattanooga, TN, USA

Sharon Glazer, PhD
University of Baltimore
Baltimore, MD, USA

Tara J. L'Heureux, PhD
University of New Haven
West Haven, CT, USA

Joseph J. Mazzola, PhD
Meredith College
Raleigh, NC, USA

Simon M. Moon, PhD
La Salle University
Philadelphia, PA, USA

Mark S. Nagy, PhD
Xavier University
Cincinnati, OH, USA

Nora P. Reilly, PhD
Radford University
Radford, VA, USA

Daniel A. Schroeder, PhD
Organization Development
Consultants, Inc.
Brookfield, WI, USA

Comila Shahani-Denning, PhD
Hofstra University
Hempstead, NY, USA

Elizabeth L. Shoenfelt, PhD
Western Kentucky University
Bowling Green, KY, USA

Judith L. Van Hein, PhD
Middle Tennessee State University
Murfreesboro, TN, USA

Susan A. Walker, MA
FedEx Freight Corporation
Germantown, TN, USA

1

An Introduction to Industrial-Organizational Psychology Master's Careers

Successful Paths to Divergent Destinations

Elizabeth L. Shoenfelt

I shall be telling this with a sigh somewhere ages and ages hence: Two roads diverged in a wood, and I—I took the one less traveled by, and that has made all the difference.

Robert Frost (1915)

At one time, earning a master's degree in industrial-organizational (I-O) psychology was likely the road less traveled; this may no longer be the case. A 2014 U.S. Bureau of Labor Statistics report identified I-O psychology as the occupation with the highest projected growth rate from 2012 to 2022 (ABC News, 2014). Again in 2018, I-O psychology was identified by the Bureau of Labor Statistics (2019) as a top job. Bailey (2020), in a recent publication of the American Psychological Association, noted that increased interest in I-O master's degrees likely is driven by higher visibility in the workplace, readily obtained jobs, interesting work, and great pay. The strong job market for I-O psychologists is predicted to remain so for at least the next decade (Bureau of Labor Statistics, 2018).

Bailey (2020) stated that "master's degrees in industrial-organizational psychology are hot" (p. 60), noting an increase in applications to I-O master's programs and growth in the number of programs to meet this demand, yet a selective applicant acceptance rate. Over the past three decades there has been substantial growth in the number of I-O psychology master's programs. In 1983, there were fewer than 15 master's I-O programs. In 1993, Lowe identified 55 master's-level I-O programs. Currently, the Society for Industrial and Organizational Psychology (SIOP)'s webpage (2019) lists over 150 non–distance-learning master's programs in I-O psychology. Most of these

Elizabeth L. Shoenfelt, *An Introduction to Industrial-Organizational Psychology Master's Careers* In: *Mastering the Job Market.* Edited by: Elizabeth L. Shoenfelt, Oxford University Press (2021). © Society of Industrial and Organizational Psychology. DOI: 10.1093/oso/9780190071172.003.0001 programs are not affiliated with a doctoral program (Koppes, 1991; SIOP, 2019). Master's programs and master's graduates outnumber their doctoral-level counterparts. Estimates based on the SIOP website suggest more than three times as many graduate each year from master's programs (1,850) as from doctoral programs (520; Shoenfelt, Stone, & Kottke, 2018). The job market for master's-level I-O psychologist is strong and their career outlook arguably is quite favorable for the foreseeable future.

This book, *Mastering the Job Market: Career Issues for Master's Level Industrial-Organizational Psychologists*, is the second on I-O master's graduates in the SIOP Professional Practice Series. The first volume, *Mastering Industrial-Organizational Psychology: Training Issues for Master's Level I-O Psychologists* (Shoenfelt, 2020), provides best practices for admission to graduate school; master's graduate program content, including curriculum, applied experiences, and thesis requirements; and faculty issues such as balancing teaching, research, service, and consulting. This volume, *Mastering the Job Market*, focuses on careers for master's-level I-O psychologists and how well master's-level training programs prepare graduates for a variety of career paths. Specific topics covered in this volume include career options for I-O master's graduates; essential knowledge, skills, and experiences; applying for and landing the first job; on- and off-boarding; professional development; and professional identity. The contributors to this volume, as with *Mastering Industrial-Organizational Psychology*, are I-O faculty members and program directors from top I-O master's programs (Acikgoz et al., 2018; Vodanovich, Morganson, & Kass, 2018).

Two surveys were conducted to provide an empirical basis for the claims made in this book, one for graduates of I-O master's programs (Shoenfelt, 2019a) and one for employers of I-O master's graduates (Shoenfelt, 2019b). The survey data offer different perspectives on career options, skills and competencies needed for these various options, and coursework and experiences most likely to impart the required knowledge, skill, and ability (KSAs) for success. I first provide a brief overview of I-O psychology and the types of activities performed by master's-level I-O psychologists before describing in detail the methodology used to develop the surveys and demographic data from each survey.

Brief Introduction to I-O Psychology

SIOP, the national organization for I-O psychologists, defines I-O psychology as the scientific study of the workplace. I-O psychologists apply the knowledge, principles, and scientific methods of psychology to issues of critical relevance to business, including talent management, coaching, assessment, selection, training, organization development, motivation, leadership, and performance (SIOP, 2019).

Specifically, I-O psychologists use science and practice to assist organizations and the people in those organizations to achieve maximum work effectiveness and to promote employee well-being in the workplace. To ensure individuals *can* perform effectively, I-O psychologists typically start with job analysis, the most foundational of I-O activities, to systematically identify the essential work requirements of a job (e.g., tasks, equipment, context) as well as the knowledge, skills, abilities, and other attributes (KSAOs) needed by the individual(s) who will perform the work. The information from the job analysis becomes the cornerstone for many I-O practices. Based on the KSAOs needed for a job, I-O psychologists develop and validate tests to identify/select job applicants who have or can develop the ability to perform the job well. Job analysis information on job requirements can be used to develop performance management systems to guide and evaluate employee performance. Both task information and KSA information are essential to developing and evaluating job training programs. Each of these personnel actions must be done within the framework of the Equal Employment Opportunity laws and guidelines. These practices all fall within the "industrial" focus of I-O psychology, also referred to as personnel psychology, and help to ensure the individual employee is capable of performing the job.

The other major area of I-O psychology, the "organizational" focus, helps to ensure the individual *will* perform the job and will remain engaged and satisfied. Organizational psychology addresses issues at the individual level, such as motivation, and attitudes, such as job satisfaction, commitment, and perceptions of fairness. At the group level, organizational psychologists work with leaders and groups, applying principles of team dynamics to ensure performance effectiveness. At the macro or organizational level, I-O psychologists apply organizational theory to ensure optimal design for organizations. Through organization development they help organizations grow and change to meet the changing demands of technology, globalization, and the products and services provided to clients and customers.

Many I-O activities require skills in both industrial *and* organizational psychology. For example, an organizational psychologist interested in measuring job satisfaction must rely on industrial psychology knowledge of psychometrics to ensure the satisfaction questionnaire is reliable and valid. An industrial psychologist conducting a job analysis study must rely on organizational skills to develop rapport with job incumbents to ensure they provide accurate information about their job. Thus, in both foci of I-O psychology, science and practice are used to ensure people in organizations can and will perform their jobs effectively and that the organization is successful.

In I-O psychology, the master's degree is primarily a practitioner's degree, with most master's-level graduates possessing technical skills similar to those of a doctoral candidate (e.g., skills in survey research, job analysis, test validation, employee selection, data analysis). Master's-level I-O practitioners tend to be quite successful in the job market, and most graduates readily find employment related to the discipline (Shoenfelt, 2019a). Further, master's graduates typically view their training as well targeted toward the skills useful for employment (Erffmeyer & Mendel, 1990; Shoenfelt, 2019a). Salaries for master's-level I-O graduates are competitive. In 2018, the Bureau of Labor Statistics identified median income for I-O psychologists as $97,260 and the median annual salary for I-O psychologists in management as $111,270.

In sum, I-O master's programs are growing in number, most graduates are finding relevant employment, and most are well paid. Clearly, those with careers in I-O psychology have a bright future ahead. Figure 1.1 illustrates the variety of job titles held by individuals with I-O master's degrees. In this book we explore the essential elements leading to a successful career in I-O psychology at the master's level.

Empirical Basis for *Mastering the Job Market*

This volume's sister work, *Mastering Industrial-Organizational Psychology: Training Issues for Master's Level I-O Psychologists* (Shoenfelt, 2020), provides a wealth of information about I-O master's graduate programs, faculty issues, and information for student advisement. Much of the content of *Mastering Industrial-Organizational Psychology* is based on the cornucopia of experiential and tacit knowledge of the 17 contributors who serve as faculty and I-O program directors at some of the top-ranked I-O master's programs in the country (Acikgoz et al., 2018; Vodanovich et al., 2018). The present volume focuses on I-O master's careers. Even though many I-O master's programs maintain good relationships with their graduates and informally track their

Figure 1.1. A word cloud based on job titles of I-O master's graduates.

career progress, there were few systematic data addressing the careers of I-O master's graduates. Accordingly, to provide an empirical basis for the content of this book, I conducted two surveys: one for graduates of I-O master's programs, the I-O Master's Graduate Survey (Shoenfelt, 2019a; subsequently "Graduate Survey"), and one for those who employ I-O master's graduates, the I-O Master's Employer Survey (Shoenfelt, 2019b; subsequently "Employer Survey"). This section details the methodology used to develop the surveys, survey administration, and respondent demographic information. The subsequent chapters in this book describe the data from both surveys in detail as they relate to each chapter's focus.

Survey Development

For both the Graduate Survey and the Employer Survey, contributing authors for this volume were invited to submit survey items to provide data for their chapter. Submitted items were edited and revised to develop the two surveys. For each survey, items addressing the same or similar content were clustered together; similar items were combined and edited. Once items were consolidated, they were again edited to ensure consistency in both the stem structure and item response format. Items addressing graduate competencies were edited to be consistent with the SIOP *Guidelines for Education and Training in Industrial-Organizational Psychology* (SIOP, 2016) at both the Core Content level and the individual competency level. The item clusters were arranged in the survey to present a coherent organization to survey respondents. I-O master's students piloted the surveys to ensure items were worded in an easily understood manner, response formats were operational, and the time to complete each survey was reasonable. Average time for completion of the pilot surveys was under 30 minutes for the Graduate Survey and under 20 minutes for the Employer Survey. Chapter authors were invited to review the surveys and to provide feedback both before they were posted to the online platform and again after the surveys were posted.

Survey Administration

There is no known comprehensive database of I-O master's graduates. Although most I-O master's graduate students belong to SIOP, far fewer maintain their membership after graduation (see Chapter 7 in this volume by Nagy, Aziz, & Schroeder), making it difficult to track I-O master's graduates. I-O graduate program directors, many of whom maintain contact with their alumni, likely were the best source for accessing I-O master's graduates to complete the survey.

I-O master's program director email addresses were harvested from the SIOP Graduate Training Program website (SIOP, 2019). A number of programs did not identify a specific individual as program director. An online search of individual program webpages for many of these programs yielded a program contact and email address. Of the 184 programs on the SIOP webpage that indicated they offered MS or MA degrees (or a MS or MA *and* a doctoral degree) in I-O psychology or another closely related field, we located contact information for 147. Some 50 programs did not indicate a delivery format on the SIOP webpage; of the 135 programs that did, most (72.5%) were brick and mortar; 17% were online only; 10.47% were combination. Of the 37 programs for which we were unable to locate a contact person/email address, 17 were international programs, 7 were multiple locations of the same school, and 5 were online programs.

On April 9, 2019, all 147 I-O master's program contact persons were sent an email invitation for their graduates and the employers of their graduates to participate in the two surveys. The email explained that the surveys were being conducted for a SIOP Professional Practice Series volume on I-O master's careers. Program directors were requested to send the URL for the Graduate Survey to their graduates and the URL for the Employer Survey to any employers of their graduates for whom they had contact information. A sample email to be forwarded to program graduates was included. This sample email asked I-O master's graduates to complete the Graduate Survey and to invite their supervisor to complete the Employer Survey. Individuals who had both earned an I-O master's degree and employed I-O master's graduates were invited to complete both surveys, but from the appropriate different perspectives. Follow-up emails were sent regularly to program directors until the final reminder was sent on May 3, 2019. Thus, survey distribution was a function of the program directors' ability and willingness to distribute the survey invitation to their program graduates. The surveys remained open online until May 15, 2019.

Graduate Survey Respondents

Program Demographics

Because this survey targeted graduates of I-O master's programs, 32 respondents who indicated they had not yet graduated from their master's program were removed from the dataset. There were 958 remaining respondents who provided valid responses; not all respondents completed the entire survey. An early survey item asked respondents to indicate the program from which they graduated; there were 944 valid responses identifying 66 different graduate programs, and the number of respondents from a given program ranged from 1 to 78 (see the appendix at the end of this chapter for the list of programs). Nine of the 14 invalid responses were names of departments or discipline (e.g., I-O Psychology or Psychology Department). The majority of respondents earned their I-O master's degree from a brick-and-mortar program (91.8%); of these, most were full-time students (89.3%) rather than part-time students (6.8%); 3.9% reported attending both full and part time. Only 2% of respondents reported completing their program fully online; 6.2% completed their degree in a combination/hybrid program. That the Graduate Survey respondents were primarily full-time students in brick-and-mortar programs is partially a function of these programs maintaining alumni contacts. That is, the program directors had contact information to invite their alumni to complete the survey.

Respondent Demographics

Of the 697 that reported gender, 41% reported male, 58.2% female, and 0.3% transgender; 0.4% preferred not to say. The majority of the 696 respondents who reported ethnicity indicated White (85.2%); 3.7% indicated Asian; 3.4% indicated Black or African American; 3.3% indicated Hispanic or Latino; 3.0% indicated two or more races; and 1.1% indicated another ethnicity. Respondent mean age was 34.96 years ($SD = 9.11$); median age was 33 years; the interquartile range was 28 to 38 years. Master's graduation year ranged from 1962 to 2018, with a median of 2013. The interquartile range for graduation year was 2007 to 2016; less than 10% of the sample graduated before 2000. Most respondents reported their undergraduate major to be psychology (75%) or a variant of psychology (14.3%; 2% reported I-O psychology); 4.3% reported a business major, and 5.3% reported another undergraduate major.

Employment Demographics

I-O master's graduates reported applying to a median of five jobs before receiving their first job offer. Many (45%) of 861 respondents reported securing their first position before graduation; 16.3% secured a position within three months of graduation, 14.6% in three to six months following graduation, and 18% reported they spent more than six months following graduation to secure their first job. Most (67.5%) of I-O master's graduates felt either extremely well prepared (27%) or prepared (40.5%) for their first job. The median reported base salary range for the first position was reported as $50,000 to $59,000 (n = 861; unadjusted for year of graduation). Respondents reported working in a mean of 2.46 organizations (SD = 1.69, n = 850). The median current base salary range was $75,000 to $100,000 (n = 843).

Respondents reported working in 41 of the 50 U.S. states, the District of Columbia, and 21 locations outside of the United States. The largest employment sector reported by the I-O master's respondents was private-sector for-profit organizations (54.9%). I-O master's graduates also were employed in consulting organizations (13.4%), nonprofit organizations (8.6%), educational institutions (8.5%), state or local governments (6.4%), federal government (2.6% military or military contractors; 2.4% non-military), and self-employed (3.1%).

Employer Survey Respondents

Respondent Demographics

Responses were obtained from 143 employers who have one or more I-O master's graduates as their direct report. Not all respondents completed all survey items. In essence, these respondent demographics describe those who supervise I-O master's graduates.

A variety of disciplines were reported by 126 employer respondents as the area in which they have their formal training/education. I-O psychology (51.6%) and I-O psychology combined with another discipline (4.7%) were the most prevalent areas of training. This reporting is consistent with the 71 affirmative responses to a single yes/no item inquiring if the individual had a degree in I-O psychology. The only other areas with more than a single respondent were variations on human resources management (8.7%), MBA and other business backgrounds (6.3%), and other areas of psychology (6.3%). Respondents reported a mean of 6.3 (SD = 6.38, n = 133) years of experience in their current position.

The mean age of employer respondents was 42.77 years (SD = 9.7, n = 90). The interquartile range for age was 35 to 49 years. Gender was about evenly split among 99 respondents, with 50.5% male, 46.5% female, and 2.1% who preferred not to say. The majority of the employer respondents were White (87.2%); 7.4% were Hispanic or Latino; 2.1% identified as two or more races;

and only 1.1%, respectively, indicated the ethnicities of Black or African American, Asian, and other.

Organizational Demographics

Employers reported working in 31 of the 50 U.S. states (n = 135), Washington, DC (n = 4), and outside of the United States (n = 2). As might be expected, the type of organization reported by 143 employers parallels the types of organizations reported by their I-O master's direct reports. The most frequent organizational setting reported by employers was private-sector for-profit organizations (47.6%). Other types of organizations included consulting organizations (18.2%), nonprofit organizations (11.2%), state or local governments (9.8%), educational institutions (8.4%), federal government (2.1% military or military contractors; 1.4% non-military), and self-employed (0.7%).

Employment of I-O Master's Graduates

When asked how many positions in their organization are filled by I-O master's graduates, the median response among 122 respondents was 4; the interquartile range was 2 to 10. The median response when asked how many of these I-O master's graduates are direct reports was one, with an interquartile range of one to two. Most (53.7%) of these same respondents indicated that there were no doctoral-level I-O psychologists in their organizations (interquartile range was zero to three doctoral-level I-O psychologists in the organization). Thus, I-O master's graduates are likely to work directly with few other I-O master's graduates, although there may be others in their organization; it is likely there will be few doctoral-level I-O psychologists in the organization.

Most of the employer respondents (85.7%; n = 133) indicated they make hiring decisions in their organization; 42.8% indicated they had hired at least one employee with a degree in I-O psychology. When asked how many applicants typically apply for an I-O–related position in their organization, the median response was 20 (n = 74); the interquartile range was 5 to 50. These same respondents indicated they typically interview a median of five individuals (interquartile range three to eight) for a position, by phone or in person. Out of 111 respondents, 58.6% indicated they hire master's-level I-O interns; the median number of interns hired was one, with an interquartile range of one to two.

Results of both the Graduate Survey and the Employer Survey are discussed in detail in the subsequent six chapters of this book. In each chapter, authors describe how they may have subsetted the survey samples described in this chapter, and the results of their analysis of the data pertaining to their chapter.

Conclusion

The future looks bright for I-O master's programs and their graduates. I-O master's programs are receiving increased attention and support from SIOP. The American Psychological Association has taken note of the growth in I-O master's programs and the success of I-O master's graduates in the job market (Bailey, 2020). The strong job market for I-O psychologists is predicted to remain so for at least the next decade (Bureau of Labor Statistics, 2018).

This volume provides important information about careers, based on nationwide surveys of I-O master's graduates and their employers, as well as insights from I-O master's faculty from top-ranked I-O master's programs (Acikgoz et al., 2018; Vodanovich et al., 2018). The remaining six chapters of this volume address a myriad of issues related to the careers of master's-level I-O psychologists. In Chapter 2, L'Heureux and Van Hein provide information about job opportunities available to I-O master's graduates. The authors draw heavily on Graduate Survey data to identify common occupational titles, organizational roles, and salary ranges for both recent I-O graduates and those later in their careers. In Chapter 3, Glazer, Moon, Ayman, and Berger take a deep dive into the Graduate Survey and Employer Survey data to identify essential competencies for success as an I-O practitioner. Next, Walker, Bartels, and Shahani-Denning provide an abundance of advice in Chapter 4 for the job search and offer specific strategies and actions for securing the first I-O position. Cunningham and Reilly then provide advice on the lifelong journey of one's career in Chapter 5, using the metaphor of the many stops on a train ride to discuss on-boarding and off-boarding processes. The authors examine formal and informal on-boarding and off-boarding for master's-level I-O psychology practitioners and provide insight into how to pursue career objectives and manage challenging career transitions. In Chapter 6, Mazzola, Chrobot-Mason, and Cox address the important postgraduate experience of continuing training and development for I-O master's graduates. The authors discuss common certifications and continuing education opportunities relevant to I-O master's-level practitioner careers. In the final chapter, Nagy, Aziz, and Schroeder discuss the professional identity of I-O master's graduates. The authors make an important distinction between licensing and certification/credentialing and argue for establishing an I-O psychology certification process. In conclusion, the authors provide suggestions for developing the professional identity of master's I-O psychology graduates in the future.

Of note, the SIOP Professional Practice Series sister volume to this book, *Mastering Industrial-Organizational Psychology: Training Issues for Master's Level I-O Psychologists* (Shoenfelt, 2020), provides a wealth of information about I-O master's programs as well as best practices for training master's-level I-O psychologists offered by faculty from top-ranked I-O master's programs (Acikgoz et al., 2018; Vodanovich et al., 2018).

Appendix

Programs with Graduates Participating in Graduate Survey

Program
Angelo State University
Appalachian State University
Austin Peay State University
Baruch College
California State University, Long Beach
California State University, San Bernardino
Capella University
Carlos Albizu University
Cleveland State University
Columbia University, Teachers College
DePaul University
East Carolina University
Eastern Kentucky University
Emporia State University
Fairleigh Dickinson University

Program

Florida Institute of Technology
Fordham University (Universidad de Atacama)
George Mason University
Grand Canyon University
Hofstra University
Illinois Institute of Technology
Illinois State University
Indiana University Purdue University Indianapolis
La Salle University
Lamar University
Middle Tennessee State University
Minnesota State University, Mankato
Missouri State University
Montclair State University
Northern Kentucky University
Radford University
Roosevelt University
San Diego State University
San Francisco State University
Southern New Hampshire University
St. Cloud State
St. Mary's University
University of Akron
University of Albany
University of Baltimore
University of Central Florida
University of Detroit
University of Detroit Mercy
University of Georgia
University of Hartford
University of Houston—Clear Lake
University of Mannheim
University of Maryland Baltimore County
University of Maryland College Park
University of Minnesota Duluth

(Continued)

Program
University of Missouri—St. Louis
University of Nebraska at Omaha
University of New Haven
University of North Carolina—Charlotte
University of North Texas
University of Tennessee at Chattanooga
University of Texas at Arlington
University of Tulsa
University of West Florida
University of Wisconsin—Madison
University of Wisconsin—Stout
Valdosta State University
West Chester University of Pennsylvania
Western Kentucky University
Wright State University
Xavier University

References

ABC News. (2014). https://abcnews.go.com/Business/americas-20-fastest-growing-jobs-surprise/story?id=22364716

Acikgoz, Y., Huelsman, T. J., Swets, J. L., Dixon, A. R., Jeffer, S. N., Olsen, D. R., & Rosset, A. (2018). The cream of the crop: Student and alumni perceptions of I-O psychology master's degree program quality. *The Industrial-Organizational Psychologist*, 55(4). http://my.siop.org/tip/jan18/editor/ArtMID/13745/ArticleID/334/The-Cream-of-the-Crop-Student-and-Alumni-Perceptions-of-I-O-Psychology-Masters-Degree-Program-Quality

Bailey, D. (2020, January/February). Special report: Top 10 trends for 2020. *Monitor on Psychology: A Publication of the American Psychological Association*, 51(1), 38–75.

Bureau of Labor Statistics. (2018, May).https://www.bls.gov/oes/current/oes193032.htm

Bureau of Labor Statistics. (2019). *Occupational employment statistics*. https://www.bls.gov/oes/current/oes193032.htm

Erffmeyer, E. S., & Mendel, R. M. (1990). Master's level training in industrial-organizational psychology: A case study of the perceived relevance of graduate training. *Professional Psychology: Research and Practice*, 21(5), 405–408.

Frost, R. (1915). *The Road Not Taken by Robert Frost*. https://www.poetryfoundation.org/poems/44272/the-road-not-taken

Koppes, L. L. (1991). I-O psychology master's level training: Reality and legitimacy in search of recognition. *The Industrial-Organizational Psychologist, 29*(2), 59–67. https://doi.org/10.1037/e579482009-010

Lowe, R. H. (1993). Master's programs in industrial-organizational psychology: Current status and a call for action. *Professional Psychology: Research and Practice, 24,* 27–34. https://doi.org/10.1037/0735-7028.24.1.27

Shoenfelt, E. L. (2019a). I-O master's graduate survey. Survey conducted for E. L. Shoenfelt (Ed.) (2021). *Mastering the job market: Career issues for master's level industrial-organizational psychologist.* New York: Oxford University Press.

Shoenfelt, E. L. (2019b). I-O master's employer survey. Survey conducted for E. L. Shoenfelt (Ed.) (2021). *Mastering the job market: Career issues for master's level industrial-organizational psychologist.* New York: Oxford University Press.

Shoenfelt, E. L. (Ed.) (2020). *Mastering industrial-organizational psychology: Training issues for master's level I-O psychologists.* New York: Oxford University Press.

Shoenfelt, E. L., Stone, N. J., & Kottke, J. L. (2018). Gaining organizational entry and developing partnerships for applied research and experience: A perspective from industrial-organizational psychology master's programs. *Industrial and Organizational Psychology: Perspectives on Science and Practice, 11,* 606–612.

Society for Industrial and Organizational Psychology, Inc. (2016). *Guidelines for education and training in industrial/organizational psychology.* Bowling Green, OH: Author. https://www.siop.org/Events-Education/Graduate-Training-Program/Guidelines-for-Education-and-Training

Society for Industrial and Organizational Psychology, Inc. (2019). *Graduate training programs in I-O psychology and related fields.* https://www.siop.org/Events-Education/Graduate-Training-Program

Vodanovich, S. J., Morganson, V. J., & Kass, S. J. (2018). Ranking I-O master's programs using objective data from I-O coordinators. *The Industrial-Organizational Psychologist, 55*(4). http://my.siop.org/tip/jan18/editor/ArtMID/13745/ArticleID/333/Ranking-I-O-Masters-Programs-Using-Objective-Data-From-I-O-Coordinators1

2

Career Outcomes for Master's-Level Industrial-Organizational Psychologists

Tara J. L'Heureux and Judith L. Van Hein

The field of industrial-organizational (I-O) psychology has focused broadly on improving the lives of employees while at the same time benefiting the organization. Much of the work I-O psychologists perform provides the foundation for sound personnel practice in organizations, such as job analysis, test development and validation, designing performance management systems, and training and development. In organizational settings, I-O psychologists hold many job titles that often do not include the term "I-O psychology." Common job titles for master's-level I-O psychologists might include organizational design and development consultant, human resources business partner, talent development manager, engagement specialist, people data analyst, director of global total rewards, compensation analyst, leadership development business partner, organizational assessment director, and a variety of other titles. Accordingly, many in the general public are not familiar with I-O psychology and the important work done by I-O psychologists to ensure organizations and the people in them are effective and successful (Gasser, Butler, Waddilove, & Tan, 2004; Ryan, 2003). In our chapter, we summarize the career options available to individuals with I-O psychology master's degrees and the type of work they perform, both at the start of their career and later on. In summarizing the results of the I-O Master's Graduate Survey (Shoenfelt, 2019a), we give guidance to students who wish to pursue graduate education in I-O at the master's level and, subsequently, careers in I-O psychology. Using the data from the Graduate Survey, we examine the major employment categories of individuals with a master's degree in I-O psychology, salary data, upward mobility, and career satisfaction.

Twenty-five years ago, Lowe (1993) noted that "on a national basis we have little systematic information about the jobs that are or might be held

Tara J. L'Heureux and Judith L. Van Hein, *Career Outcomes for Master's-Level Industrial-Organizational Psychologists*
In: *Mastering the Job Market*. Edited by: Elizabeth L. Shoenfelt, Oxford University Press (2021). © Society of Industrial and Organizational Psychology. DOI: 10.1093/oso/9780190071172.003.0002

by master's graduates in I-O" (p. 31) and argued that systematic attention should be paid to issues of education, employment, and professional identity for master's graduates in I-O psychology. Two decades later, we continue to have limited understanding of the career outcomes and pathways of master's graduates. The need for such employment and career-related information becomes apparent when one considers the dramatic increase in I-O master's programs and large numbers of graduates entering professional practice. Kottke, Shoenfelt, and Stone (2014) reported that 1,850 master's degrees in I-O psychology are earned each year from 159 I-O psychology programs, over three times the number of I-O doctoral degrees granted (530). More recently, Islam, Chetta, Martins, van Govan, Kozikowski, and Needhammer (2018) estimated that, in 2016, the number of I-O master's degree graduates exceeded doctoral-level graduates by a factor of 4.5. Given that the requirement of a doctoral degree for academic positions precludes employment for all but a few I-O master's graduates, the master's degree is essentially a practitioner degree and is currently the most visible face of the field (Weathington, Bergman, & Bergman, 2014).

One goal of this chapter is to identify the job types and work activities of those who hold an I-O psychology master's degree; we map these data onto familiar occupational and career frameworks. A second goal is to investigate the career success of I-O graduates by describing both objective and subjective measures typically used for this purpose. Third, two factors, respondents' perceptions of career success and the relatedness of career to degree and perceived employability, are examined as important drivers of perceived value of the I-O psychology master's degree.

Career Outcomes of Master's I-O Psychology Graduates

Little published information exists on the career outcomes and pathways of master's-level I-O practitioners. Schippmann, Hawthorne, and Schmitt (1992a) compared the types of jobs held by master's-level and doctoral graduates of I-O psychology programs. Although some overlap existed between the two groups in industry settings (e.g., organization development), master's graduates exclusively populated the compensation, training, data analysis, and personnel job types. Further, within these job types, some reported work activities were "outside of what might be considered traditional I-O job content areas" (Schippmann, Schmitt, & Hawthorne, 1992b, p. 37).

Member employment data reported by the Society for Industrial and Organizational Psychology (SIOP; siop.org/Career-Center) provided some insight into the types of jobs held by master's graduates. Zelin et al. (2015) presented a career path framework that included government, industry, consulting, and academia employment sectors. The data show that master's and doctoral graduates are employed in vastly different areas; for example, the industry sector represented the largest category for master's-level graduates and also included the fewest doctoral graduates. The use of SIOP member data to track I-O master's career outcomes is problematic. Although many master's graduate students are SIOP members, few master's graduates maintain their SIOP membership (see Chapter 7 in this volume by Nagy, Aziz, & Schroeder). For many years, SIOP restricted its membership to individuals with doctoral degrees. Even though SIOP created a pathway to full membership for master's-level I-O graduates in 2015 (SIOP, 2019), information about I-O psychology master's graduates is very limited.

Knowledge about career outcomes for graduates of I-O master's programs will benefit multiple stakeholders. For academic programs, career outcome data are necessary to determine the extent to which the I-O psychology master's degree is meeting the needs not only of graduates, but also of professional practice. Career outcome information can inform curriculum content, co-curricular experiences, and the competencies most beneficial to I-O graduates. The literature on I-O master's graduates has largely focused on the relevance and quality of master's-level training in I-O psychology, particularly in reference to the SIOP (2016) *Guidelines for Education and Training in Industrial-Organizational Psychology* (Tett, Walser, Brown, Simonet, & Tonidandel, 2013; Trahan & McAllister, 2002), where curricula of graduate programs are compared to the heavily content-focused education and training guidelines. Determining the extent to which the education and training of master's-level graduates is relevant to the knowledge, skills, and abilities needed to succeed in 21st-century professional roles provides value beyond traditional content approaches to assessing the quality of education and training. In this chapter we document the types of jobs graduates obtain and specify the nature of the work activities performed across different jobs. Having a clear idea of where graduates work and what they do is important, as work setting is an important determinant of professional identity (Ryan & Ford, 2010). Describing career outcomes achieved by graduates of I-O psychology master's programs is one step of many to enhance the visibility of the field in general and of the largest group applying I-O psychology concepts in organizational settings.

Empirical Data on I-O Master's Career Outcomes

The Graduate Survey (Shoenfelt, 2019a) provided data on employment outcomes of I-O master's graduates that serve as objective indicators of career success and career progression.

Defining Our Sample

In this chapter, our overarching focus was to describe the pre- and post-degree work experiences and career outcomes of master's-level practitioners in I-O psychology. We excluded those respondents who held a doctoral degree, who were in progress for an advanced degree, or who did not respond to the items about additional degrees earned or degrees in progress. We excluded respondents who earned degrees in unrelated fields (e.g., MS in cell biology). Eighty-three respondents were deleted from the analysis. The remaining sample consisted of respondents who held a master's degree in I-O psychology and had not earned another degree or were not enrolled in another degree program. Less than 5% of survey participants went on to earn a doctoral degree. Table 2.1 presents the percentage of our sample at early, mid, and late career stage and the median age of each cohort.

Job Types and Work Activities

The dearth of information about the work of master's-level I-O psychologists prompted us to gather detailed information about the types of jobs they obtained and their work activities. We use several frameworks, each with

Table 2.1 Percentage of Participants by Years Since Earning Master's Degree

Years Since Master's Degree	Percentage of Sample (n = 909)	Median Age (n = 642)
1–3 years	32%	27
4–8 years	30%	31
9–15 years	23%	36
16+ years	15%	47

a different focus, to provide alternate views of respondents' jobs. We describe master's-level employment by summarizing the graduates' work experiences, such as types of jobs held, work activities, salary, and career progression. Similar to recent research on the occupations of U.S. psychology baccalaureates (Rajecki, 2012), we examine the extent to which I-O psychology master's graduates' employment is dispersed across a broad range of occupations, and to what extent the occupations are similar to each other. Further, we compare and contrast our classification of jobs to those put forth by others (e.g., SIOP's career study; Zelin et al., 2015).

Pre-Degree Experiences

Several survey items addressed respondents' experience while in graduate school that may be related to their career outcomes. For example, items addressed perceptions of available career options, internship experiences, and the extent to which respondents felt prepared for their first position after graduate school. All ratings were made on a 5-point Likert-type scale.

Overall, 81% of master's graduates completed an internship and the majority of the internships were paid. In addition, 31% of those who completed an internship got their first professional job with the same organization. Surprisingly, a higher percentage, 27%, of recent graduates (one to three years since graduation) did not complete an internship, although 73% of recent graduates did complete one. Among those who completed an internship, 80% reported they either agreed or strongly agreed with the statement "My internship prepared me for my first job" and 64% agreed with the statement "Internship helped define my career path." Together, these two items represent the utility of the internship experience in terms of preparation and fit with career. Alumni reported having a good understanding of potential careers whether they had an internship or not. Many employers, however, value applicants with internship experience. The majority (69%) of employers surveyed in the Employer Survey (Shoenfelt, 2019b) agreed that internships were an important or very important consideration in the hiring process. Therefore, students should be strongly encouraged or required to complete an internship as part of the I-O psychology master's degree.

In general, master's graduates were moderately aware of the career options available to them ($M = 3.8$, $SD = .96$, $n = 827$). Overall, master's programs appeared to be successful in preparing graduates for employment. Seventy-five percent of graduates reported they felt prepared or extremely prepared for their first job. Many respondents (47%) secured their first I-O related position before they received their master's degree.

Occupational Classification of First and Current Jobs

Graduate Survey respondents reported the functional job title of their first full-time position after receiving their master's degree and their current position, as well as the level of both positions (e.g., assistant, director, specialist, business partner). We compared employment outcomes for respondents' first and current positions. Job titles and levels were instrumental descriptors for placing jobs within occupational classifications such as O*NET, as well as the I-O career framework put forth by Zelin et al. (2015) and currently used by SIOP on its webpage (siop.org/Career-Center). We applied the Standard Occupation Classification (SOC) system to classify respondents' first and current jobs into occupational categories with unique SOC codes. For example, the job title "learning and development specialist" mapped to Training and Development Specialists (SOC 13-1151.00), part of the "Business and Financial Operations." In addition to job content information, job titles often implied a rank or hierarchy within an organization. For example, job titles such as "people development director" were mapped to the Training and Development Managers (SOC 11-3131.00) occupation. Two I-O psychology faculty coders reached consensus on the SOCs of 806 of the 875 valid respondents' first job titles.

In addition, as needed, the two coders used another tool, O*NET SOC Autocoder, an online tool developed to sort job titles into established SOC codes. We mapped 736 first job titles into O*NET categories related to the field of I-O psychology. Examples of O*NET job titles deemed unrelated to I-O psychology included personal financial advisors, clinical research coordinators, and sales engineers. Two job classifications, Management Analysts and I-O Psychologists, overlapped a substantial degree in sample titles, tasks, and work activities. For example, both occupations included the titles of management consultant, organizational development consultant, and organizational consultant. Work activities and tasks were similar for the two occupations; however, career descriptors for I-O Psychologists included tasks with an external orientation (e.g., "confer with clients to exchange information" and "conduct presentations on research findings for clients"). We used this external client focus to classify external management consulting into the I-O Psychologist occupation and internal management consultants into the Management Analyst occupation.

First Position

As Table 2.2 indicates, I-O psychology master's graduates entered the workforce in a variety of jobs, with more than 80% in the Business and Financial Operations (SOC 13-0000.00) job family that included Human Resources Specialists (SOC 13-1071.00); Management Analysts (SOC 13-1111.00); Training and Development Specialists (SOC 13-1151.00); and Compensation, Benefits, and Job Analysis Specialists (SOC 13-1141.00). The primary organizing principle of the SOC job family system is work performed, meaning that jobs families have similar generalized work activities (e.g., establishing and maintaining interpersonal relationships) and detailed work activities (e.g., training to enhance job skills).

A smaller percentage (11.7%) of respondent first jobs belonged to the Life, Physical, and Social Science job family (SOC 19-0000.00), and included jobs such as I-O Psychologists (SOC 19-3032.00) and Survey Researchers (SOC 19-3022.00). These occupations tend to focus on research and/or client orientations, but they also share many work activities and tasks with the occupations related to human resources roles described earlier. Another job family emerged in our analysis, Management (SOC 11-0000.00), which included human resources–related jobs such as Human Resources Managers (SOC 11-3121.00) and Training and Development Managers (SOC 11-3131.00). Not surprisingly, the percentage of first jobs in the management job family was small (3.9%). The O*NET framework indicated two primary areas of entry-level employment for masters-level graduates: human resources and related jobs (e.g., training, compensation) and jobs involving data gathering and analysis to solve organizational problems, often for external stakeholders (e.g., consulting positions).

Current Position

As with the analysis for first I-O-related jobs for I-O master's graduates, we used the SOC system to group current jobs into occupational categories. Our classification of current jobs resulted in a group of job families almost identical to our classification of first jobs. We were able to code 757 current job titles; 613 of these could be categorized into SOC categories related to I-O psychology. As shown in Table 2.2, the majority of

Table 2.2 O*NET Classification of First (n = 736) and Current (n = 613) Job Titles

SOC	O*NET Job Titles	First Job		Current Job	
		n	%	n	%
Business and Financial Operations					
13-1141.00	Compensation, Benefits, and Job Analysis Specialists	37	5.03	19	3.10
13-1041.00	Compliance Officers	0	0.00	6	0.98
13-1141.00	Equal Opportunity Representatives and Officers	3	0.41	0	0.00
13-1071.00	Human Resources Specialists	334	45.38	173	28.22
13-1075.00	Labor Relations Specialists	1	0.14	0	0.00
13-1111.00	Management Analysts	155	21.06	78	12.72
13-1151.00	Training and Development Specialists	55	7.47	46	7.50
Computer and Mathematical					
15-2041.00	Statisticians	5	0.68	14	2.28
Education, Training, and Library					
25-9031.01	Instructional Designers and Technologists	6	0.82	1	0.16
25-1199.00	Postsecondary Teachers, All Other	0	0.00	1	0.16
Life, Physical, and Social Sciences					
19-3032.00	Industrial-Organizational Psychologists	65	8.83	113	18.43
19-4099.01	Quality Control Analysts	10	1.36	3	0.49
19-4061.00	Social Science Research Assistants	1	0.14	1	0.16
19-3022.00	Survey Researchers	10	1.36	5	0.82
Management					
11-3111.00	Compensation and Benefits Managers	0	0.00	11	1.79
11-9033.00	Education Administrators, Postsecondary	0	0.00	1	0.16
11-3121.01	Human Resources Managers	21	2.85	110	17.94

(*Continued*)

Table 2.2 Continued

SOC	O*NET Job Titles	First Job		Current Job	
		n	%	n	%
11-3051.01	Quality Control Systems Managers	2	0.27	1	0.16
11-3131.00	Training and Development Managers	10	1.36	29	4.73
Office and Administrative Support					
43-4161.00	Human Resources Assistants, Except Payroll and Timekeeping	10	1.36	0	0.00
43-9111.00	Statistical Assistants	2	0.27	1	0.16

current job titles mapped to the Business and Financial Operations job family (51.9%) in Human Resources or related positions; 25.8% were categorized in the Management job family, also in Human Resources or related functional areas. The smallest grouping of jobs mapped to the job family titled Life, Physical, and Social Sciences, and included many with external consulting jobs.

First and Current Job Levels

Most of our sample entered their first job as individual contributors (92.9%). Across all respondents, the most common first job level reported was analyst (38.3%), followed by specialist (31.5%). Similarly, for recent graduates (i.e., one to three years since degree), the most common job levels were analyst (27.6%) and specialist (27.6%). Among individual contributors at mid-career (9 to 15 years since degree), the most common job level was business partner/ consultant (35.6%). Consultant level, which included business partner and senior advisor titles in industry, is generally viewed as a high-level entry point for early careers, and was reported as the first position by 12.7% of respondents. Titles that conveyed lower-level administrative positions such as assistant, coordinator, and representative made up 10.5% of first job levels; only 7.1% entered their first I-O related positions as a manager. As years since graduation increased, the percentage of respondents in managerial

Table 2.3 Level of Position by Years Since Degree

Role	1–3 Years (n = 201)	4–8 Years (n = 190)	9–15 Years (n = 139)	16+ Years (n = 83)	Total
Individual contributor	86.57%	69.47%	43.17%	40.96%	65.25%
Manager	13.43%	30.53%	56.83%	59.04%	34.75%

positions increased. Only 13% of those who received their degree in the past 3 years were managers, whereas almost 60% of those who graduated more than 16 years ago reported managerial job titles such as director and regional manager. Table 2.3 presents percentage of those in individual contributor and manager positions by years since earning their I-O master's degree.

First and Current Base Salaries

I-O master's graduates (n = 684) reported the base salary of their first position by choosing one of 10 salary categories, and the base salary of their current position by choosing one of 11 salary categories. Naturally, starting salaries were influenced by when students graduated and accepted their first career-relevant position. Within those respondents who graduated in the last three years, the median starting salary was $50,000 to $59,000, with 61% starting with a salary between $40,000 and $79,000. There are regional differences in starting salary; 30% of recent graduates earning over $70,000 were in California. As expected, Table 2.4 indicates that lower first salaries were associated with greater number of years since degree: For instance, for those who earned their degrees more than 16 years ago, the median starting salary range was $30,000 to $39,000.

More than 700 respondents who were employed full time provided information about their current salary. Salary was clearly related to career stage. As expected, those earning the highest salaries were those who obtained their I-O master's degree 16 years ago or more. Table 2.4 shows salary ranges by years since degree for terminal master's graduates employed full time in I-O psychology–related jobs.

Table 2.4 Salaries of First Job (n = 684) and Current Job (n = 579) by Years Since Degree

Salary Range	Years Since Degree			
	1–3 Years (n = 212)	4–8 Years (n = 216)	9–15 Years (n = 154)	16+ Years (n = 102)
First Job				
Less than $20,000	0.00%	0.46%	0.00%	4.90%
$20,000–$29,999	0.47%	0.00%	2.60%	24.51%
$30,000–$39,999	4.25%	10.65%	18.18%	28.43%
$40,000–$49,999	17.92%	31.48%	[33.77%]	[23.53%]
$50,000–$59,999	[31.13%]	[28.24%]	21.43%	8.82%
$60,000–$69,999	25.94%	17.59%	16.23%	4.90%
$70,000–$79,999	14.62%	7.41%	5.84%	1.96%
$80,000–$89,999	3.77%	3.24%	1.95%	1.96%
$90,000–$99,000	0.94%	0.93%	0.00%	0.98%
More than $99,000	0.94%	0.00%	0.00%	0.00%
Current Job				
$30,001–$50,000	11.40%	2.70%	2.34%	1.37%
$50,001–$75,000	[54.40%]	26.49%	16.41%	6.85%
$75,001–$100,000	25.91%	[41.62%]	18.75%	19.18%
$100,001–$125,000	7.25%	19.46%	[25.78%]	17.81%
$125,001–$150,000	0.52%	7.57%	14.84%	[13.70%]
$150,001–$175,000	0.00%	0.54%	11.72%	10.96%
$175,001–$200,000	0.52%	1.08%	3.91%	4.11%
More than $200,000	0.00%	0.54%	6.25%	26.03%

Note: The bracketed salary range contains the 50th percentile.

Career Roles

We developed a parsimonious framework that focuses on primary roles, without regard to organizational rank, to classify first and current positions of I-O master's graduates. The resulting framework consisted of six roles—Human Resources, Training, Compensation, Organization Development, Research and Analytics—as well as an External Consulting role that cut across several work domains. For example, O*NET job categories specialist and managerial levels were collapsed across rank for the Training, Human

Resources, and Compensation occupational categories; thus, training specialists and training managers were consolidated into the "Training" role. In addition, labor relations specialists and Equal Opportunity representatives and officers were combined into the "Human Resources" role; instructional designers and technologists were placed into the "Training" role; job titles that indicated a heavy data, analytical, or research focus were placed in the "Research and Analytics" role. The "Organization Development" career role comprised most of the respondents placed in the Management Analyst O*NET occupation. Similar to the criteria used by Zelin et al. (2015), in the Consulting role we included only those who indicated both an external consulting role and working in a consulting organization.

Table 2.5 indicates that the majority of master's-level I-O graduate entry-level roles and current roles are related to Human Resources, very broadly defined, consistent with what has been reported by other sources (Shoptaugh, 2015). The practices of I-O psychology and human resources are closely aligned at the master's level and the job titles of I-O graduates' first positions reflect that shared focus (see Tables 2.2 and 2.5). SIOP and the Society for Human Resource Management (SHRM) have collaborated on a series of white papers on trends important to both fields, such as talent analytics and nonstandard work arrangements. The required emphasis on statistics, data analytics, and research methods in most I-O master's programs (Gasser et al., 2004) indicates that master's-level I-O psychologists have the potential to make meaningful contributions to addressing contemporary challenges associated with the changing nature of work.

Table 2.5 First (n = 736) and Current (n = 613) Career Roles

Career Roles	First Job		Current Job	
	n	%	n	%
Compensation	37	5.03	30	4.89
External Consulting	65	8.83	113	18.43
Human Resources	373	50.68	253	41.27
Organization Development	71	9.65	62	10.11
Research & Analytics	119	16.17	79	12.89
Training	71	9.65	76	12.40

Comparison with SIOP Careers Study

Finally, we classified current employment using the career path framework described in the recent *SIOP Careers Study* (Zelin et al., 2015), which identified four categories best described as employment sectors or organization types: government, industry, consulting, and academia. Nonprofit and for-profit organizations made up the Industry path, and local and federal government were combined into the Government path. Academia included faculty positions, but not positions in educational settings such as institutional researchers or admissions staff. Consulting included external consultants only.

Table 2.6 presents a comparison of the career paths of doctoral and master's graduates from the Zelin et al. (2015b) SIOP membership study to the career paths of our broader sample of I-O master's graduates. At the master's level, the relative ranking of employment sectors from our sample was similar to the SIOP member sample. The largest concentration of master's graduates was in the industry sector in both the SIOP sample (46%) and our sample (70%). As expected, the academic career path was poorly represented in both master's-level samples.

The career profiles of doctoral-level graduates show that 75% were classified as either academic (43%) or consulting (32%) paths; only 19% reported employment in industry. A comparison of employment sectors by degree shows what others noted decades ago (Schippmann et al., 1992b): Master's-level graduates and doctoral-level graduates have very different career outcomes. Although much has been written about consulting and academic careers of I-O doctoral graduates, we know little about the practice of I-O psychology in industry, work that is overwhelmingly performed by

Table 2.6 Comparison Between SIOP Careers Study (PhD, n = 1,176; Master's, n = 251) and Current Study (n = 613)

| | SIOP Careers Study | | | | Current Study | |
| | PhD degree | | Master's degree | | Master's degree | |
	n	%	n	%	n	%
Industry	229	19.4	119	47.5	427	69.66
Government	70	6.0	23	9.1	73	11.91
Consulting	374	31.8	96	38.2	112	18.27
Academia	503	42.8	13	5.2	1	0.16

master's-level graduates. It's important to go beyond identifying employment sectors and career roles to determine more precisely the work activities performed by I-O master's graduates. In the next section of this chapter, we describe work activities reported by Graduate Survey respondents.

Characteristics of Current Employment of I-O Master's Graduates

In this section, we explore in more detail current employment of I-O master's graduates. More than 96% of I-O master's graduate respondents indicated they were employed. An overwhelmingly majority indicated full-time employment (91.8%); few reported that they were self-employed (2.6%) or employed part time (1.9%). Among the few indicating unemployment (3.7%), only 1.4% were actively seeking employment, with the remainder reporting that they were unemployed by choice for a variety of reasons (e.g., retirement, enrollment in school, stay-at-home parent).

Sector and Industry

Most I-O psychology master's graduates are currently employed in for-profit, private-sector organizations (56.2%), followed by consulting organizations (14.2%), nonprofit organizations (8.90%), state or local governments (7.5%), and educational institutions (6.0%). We categorized the industry in which I-O master's graduates worked using the North American Industrial Classification System (NAICS), the federal government's economic classification system. I-O psychology master's graduates are currently employed across a variety of industries, including Professional Scientific and Technological Services (23.1%), Public Administration (11.4%), Finance and Insurance (10.6%), and Health Care and Social Assistance (9.8%). These four employment sectors together accounted for 54.8% of the industries where respondents were employed.

Work Activities

Our I-O master's survey respondents selected 3 work areas from a list of 18 to best describe the work performed in their current roles. Table 2.7 summarizes

Table 2.7 Work Activities by Career Role

Career Roles and Work Activities	n	Percent
Human Resources	427	42.53%
Talent management/leadership development	63	14.75%
Employee selection	40	9.37%
Organizational development/surveys	37	8.67%
External Consulting	181	18.03%
Consulting	68	37.57%
Data analytics	21	11.60%
Employee selection	15	8.29%
Training	127	12.65%
Learning and development	51	40.16%
Talent management/leadership development	32	25.20%
Organizational development/surveys	21	16.54%
Organization Development	122	12.15%
Organizational development/surveys	34	27.87%
Consulting	24	19.67%
Talent management/leadership development	20	16.39%
Research & Analytics	116	11.55%
Data analytics	39	33.62%
Research	17	14.66%
Human resources information systems	13	11.21%
Compensation	31	3.09%
Compensation & benefits/total rewards	20	64.52%
Data analytics	4	12.90%
Human resources information systems	2	6.45%

the most frequently reported work activities within various career roles. Overall, the top five areas of work activities across career roles were consulting (14.1%), talent management (12.8%), data analytics (11.8%), organization development (11.4%), and learning and development (10.7%). These findings likely reflect current trends in human resources and I-O psychology; that is, a continuing organizational focus on talent management and data analytics.

How do work activities differ across career roles? As might be expected, the work activities that were similar to the general content domain of the career role were aligned. For example, the work activity "learning and development" was heavily represented within the training role, and compensation and benefits work was represented in the compensation role. Interestingly, human resource generalist and personnel administration/policy work were not one of the top three or even top five work activities for those in human resource roles. This underscores that human resource roles performed by I-O master's graduates are largely specialist roles that are aligned with current business challenges and less administrative than traditional human resource roles. The primary work activities of I-O master's graduates are in line with many of the core content areas and skills identified in the SIOP *Guidelines for Education and Training in Industrial-Organizational Psychology* (2016), and reported work activities re- · flect a strong emphasis on research and data analytic skills.

Career Success

In this section, we examine the career success of I-O master's graduates with two related but separate sets of indicators. Our goal is to describe the characteristics of I-O master's graduate employment in terms of careers outcomes, as well as determine the drivers of career success. We use objective career success indicators such as salary gain and hierarchical advancement (Hogan, Chamorro-Premuzic, & Kaiser, 2013), in addition to subjective career success indicators such as satisfaction with income, advancement, and career (Ng, Eby, Sorensen, & Feldman, 2005). Objective career success is externally normed (e.g., Do graduates move into higher levels in the organizational hierarchy as their careers progress?) as compared to subjective career success represented by perceptions of satisfaction with their career progression. Examining both types of career success permits a more holistic review of graduates' career outcomes (Olson & Schultz, 2013) and provides a comprehensive picture of career outcomes of relatively understudied I-O master's practitioners. The Graduate Survey data enabled us to paint an in-depth portrait of the I-O professionals who received training at the master's level as preparation for employment in the field.

Career Satisfaction

I-O master's graduates reported very high levels of career satisfaction on our measure of perceptions of career success (i.e., ratings on a 5-point Likert-type scale; Greenhaus, Parasuraman, & Wormley, 1990). Participants largely attribute their career success to their I-O master's degree ($M = 4.3$, $SD = .93$, n = 805). The majority of respondents were satisfied or very satisfied with their career progression ($M = 4.25$, $SD = .93$, n = 804), and the success they've achieved in their career ($M = 4.25$, $SD = .93$, n = 804). Satisfaction with goals for advancement ($M = 4.11$, $SD = .97$, n = 804) and goals for income ($M = 4.13$, $SD = 1.04$, n = 801) also were high. Satisfaction with salary was more varied, but on average, respondents agreed they were satisfied with their salary ($M = 3.91$, $SD = 1.14$, n = 801).

Perceived Value of I-O Master's Degree in Career Success

Previous research on the employment of psychology graduates has shown that relatedness of degree to employment predicts perceptions of workforce readiness (preparedness), career satisfaction, and future job prospects (Borden & Rajecki, 2000). We examined how perceptions of relatedness of degree to graduates' jobs influence subjective career success and if greater congruence between graduate training and employment leads to increased objective and subjective career success. I-O master's graduates reported they had been able to apply what they learned in their master's program in the positions they have held ($M = 4.41$, $SD = .79$, n = 806); this was true whether they were recent graduates or had been out more than 16 years. Sixty-eight percent of all participants, regardless of career stage, reported that their job content was very or moderately related to their I-O degree.

As alumni of I-O master's programs progress in their careers, they increasingly report that their careers are unrelated or only slightly related to their I-O master's degree. Only 13% of early career I-O master's (1 to 3 years since graduation) reported that their degree was unrelated or only slightly related to their job; 21% of graduates who were 9 to 15 years postgraduation and 25% of graduates who are 16+ years postgraduation report having a job that is less related to their I-O master's degree. Self-reported job title indicates that approximately 20% of the latter group had risen to director level or above in a human resource–related area.

I-O master's graduate satisfaction with career success was positively correlated with ratings of how related their current job was to their I-O degree ($r = .43$, $p < .001$) and perceptions of employability ($r = .41$, $p < .001$) and was strongly related to the perceived value of the I-O master's degree ($r = .55$, $p <$

.001). Perceived employability was strongly linked to the perceived value of the master's degree ($r = .74$, $p < .001$). Not surprisingly, the more their current job was related to their degree, the more they perceived its value ($r = .24$, $p < .01$).

Perceived Employability

Graduate employability is an important objective for most academic programs and is clearly a relevant issue for terminal master's graduates of I-O psychology degree programs. Perceived employability is the belief that an individual has the competencies and characteristics needed to find and maintain the type of employment desired (Rothwell & Arnold, 2007). Van der Heijde and Van der Heijden (2006) found that perceived employability predicted both objective and subjective career success. We examined similar relationships in our I-O master's sample; further, we explored the connections among career outcomes with perceptions of the utility and value of their master's degree. Survey items were based on an employability measure developed by Rothwell and Arnold (2007). I-O master's survey respondents reported high levels of self-perceived employability. They felt strongly that they would be able to easily get a similar job ($M = 4.32$, $SD = .91$, n = 801) and perceived that they would be highly sought after by employers because the skills and knowledge they possess ($M = 4.27$, $SD = .81$, n = 802).

Career and Employment Sector Mobility

To describe the career paths of master's-level degree practitioners, we used a set of questions developed by Lyons, Schweitzer, and Ng (2015) to determine career mobility, defined as movement across jobs, organizations, and careers. Most I-O master's graduates (86%) reported at least one upward career move. As expected, as seen in Table 2.8, the number of upward moves increased with number of years since degree. About 30% reported lateral movement, with the modal number of lateral moves at one move (20%). Only 15% indicated downward movement, with the modal number of downward moves at one. Most of the recent graduates were still in their first job, yet 40% reported at least one promotion. Median number of positions held since graduating largely reflected career stage. Most recent graduates were in their first job,

Table 2.8 Number of Upward Career Moves by Master's Graduates

Years Since Degree	n	Mean	SD
1–3 years	186	1.15	1.06
4–8 years	173	2.18	1.33
9–15 years	131	3.05	1.65
16+ years	77	4.00	2.41
Overall	567	2.29	

but the median number of I-O–related positions held for those 9 to 15 years since graduation was four. As noted in Zelin et al. (2015), some organizations are large enough to offer an internal career ladder, but many individuals carve out a specialist role in these organizations. In addition, for those working in consulting firms, the number of promotional opportunities may be limited. As noted earlier, Table 2.4 illustrates salary progression over time, which is another marker of objective career success.

Zelin et al. (2015) reported little career movement across the four organizational categories of industry, consulting, government, and academics. The Graduate Survey data indicated that 25% of respondents had experience working in an employment sector different from the one in which they were currently employed. The most common movement reported was government to industry (28%), followed by consulting to industry (24%), and industry to consulting (20%). The least common movements were consulting to government (2.6%) and industry to academia (0.27%).

Conclusion

We described the characteristics of jobs held by master's-level I-O psychologists in rich detail based on the data from the I-O Master's Graduate Survey (Shoenfelt, 2019a). The vast majority of I-O psychology master's graduates are working in the field in positions related to their degree. The positions held cover a wide range of very broadly defined human resource–related roles. Data on employment and salary are strong indicators of the value of the I-O master's degree. Individuals with master's degrees in I-O psychology have a variety of available career paths and have the potential for upward mobility. I-O master's graduates are overwhelmingly satisfied with their career success and clearly value their I-O master's degree, whether they are recent graduates or have more than a decade of experience.

References

Borden, V. M. H., & Rajecki, D. W. (2000). First-year employment outcomes of psychology baccalaureates: First-year employment relatedness, preparedness, and prospects. *Teaching of Psychology, 27*, 164–168. doi:10.1207/s15328023top2703_01

Gasser, M., Butler, A., Waddilove, L., & Tan, R. (2004). Defining the profession of industrial-organizational psychology. *The Industrial-Organizational Psychologist, 42*(2), 15–20. doi:10.1037/e578782011-002

Greenhaus, J. H., Parasuraman, S., & Wormley, W. M. (1990). Effects of race on organizational experiences, job performance evaluations and career outcomes. *Academy of Management Journal, 33*(1), 64–86. doi:10.5465/256352

Hogan, R., Chamorro-Premuzic, T., & Kaiser, R. (2013). Employability and career success: Bridging the gap between theory and reality. *Industrial and Organizational Psychology: Perspectives on Research and Practice, 6*, 3–16. doi:10.1111/iops.12001

Islam, S., Chetta, M. H., Martins, A., van Govan, D., Kozikowski, A., & Needhammer, J. (2018). The scientist–practitioner gap among master's level I-O psychology practitioners: A text-analytic exploration. *Industrial-Organizational Psychologist, 55*(3). https://touroscholar.touro.edu/cgi/viewcontent.cgi?article=1047&context=dbs_pubs

Kottke, J. L., Shoenfelt, E. L., & Stone, N. J. (2014). Educating industrial-organizational psychologists: Lessons learned from master's programs. *Industrial and Organizational Psychology: Perspectives on Research and Practice, 7*, 26–31. doi:10.1111/iops.12099

Lowe, R. H. (1993). Master's programs in industrial-organizational psychology: Current status and a call for action. *Professional Psychology: Research and Practice, 24*, 27–34. doi:10.1037/ 0735-7028.24.1.27

Lyons, S., Schweitzer, L., & Ng, E. (2015). How have careers changed? An investigation of changing career patterns across four generations. *Journal of Managerial Psychology, 30*, 8–21. doi:10.1108/jmp-07-2014-0210

Ng, T. W. H., Eby, L. T., Sorensen, K. L., & Feldman, D. C. (2005). Predictors of objective and subjective career success: A meta-analysis. *Personnel Psychology, 58*, 367–408. doi:10.1111/j.1744-6570.2005.00515

Rajecki, D. W. (2012). Psychology baccalaureates at work: Major area subspecializations, earnings, and occupations. *Teaching of Psychology, 39*, 185–189. https://doi.org/ 10.1177/0098628312450431

Rothwell, A., & Arnold, J. (2007). Self-perceived employability: Development and validation of a scale. *Personnel Review, 36*(1), 23–41. doi:10.1108/00483480710716704

Ryan, A. M. (2003). Defining ourselves: I-O psychology's identity quest. *The Industrial-Organizational Psychologist, 41*(1), 21–33.

Ryan, A. M., & Ford, J. K. (2010). Organizational psychology and the tipping point of professional identity. *Industrial and Organizational Psychology: Perspectives on Science and Practice, 3*, 241–258. doi:10.1111/j.1754-9434.2010.01233.x

Schippmann, J. S., Hawthorne, S. L., & Schmitt, S. D. (1992a). Work roles and training needs for the practice of industrial-organizational psychology at the master's and PhD level. *Journal of Business and Psychology, 6,* 311–331. doi:10.1007/bf01126768

Schippmann, J. S., Schmitt, S. D., & Hawthorne, S. L. (1992b). I-O work roles: PhD vs. master's level practitioners. *The Industrial/Organizational Psychologist, 29*(4), 35–39.

Shoenfelt, E. L. (2019a). I-O master's graduate survey. Survey conducted for E. L. Shoenfelt (Ed.) (2021). *Mastering the job market: Career issues for master's level industrial-organizational psychologists.* New York: Oxford University Press.

Shoenfelt, E. L. (2019b). I-O master's employer survey. Survey conducted for E. L. Shoenfelt (Ed.) (2021). *Mastering the job market: Career issues for master's level industrial-organizational psychologists.* New York: Oxford University Press.

Shoenfelt, E. L., Stone, N. J., & Kottke, J. L. (2018). Gaining organizational entry and developing partnerships for applied research and experience: A perspective from industrial-organizational psychology master's programs. *Industrial and Organizational Psychology: Perspectives on Science and Practice, 11,* 606–612. doi.org/10.1017/iop.2018.122

Shoptaugh, C. (2015, August). *An evaluation of the master's program in industrial/organizational psychology: Results of the 2015 survey of alumni from the I-O track of the M.S. in Psychology Program at Missouri State University.*

Society for Industrial and Organizational Psychology, Inc. (2016). *Guidelines for education and training in industrial-organizational psychology.* Bowling Green, OH: Author.

Society for Industrial and Organizational Psychology, Inc. (2019). https://www.siop.org/Membership/Associate-to-Member

Tett, R. P., Walser, B., Brown, C., Simonet, D. V., & Tonidandel, S. (2013). 2011 SIOP graduate program benchmarking survey: Part 3: Curriculum and competencies. *The Industrial-Organizational Psychologist, 50*(4), 69–90. doi:10.1037/e559272013-007

Trahan, W. A., & McAllister, H. A. (2002). Master's level training in industrial/organizational psychology: Does it meet the SIOP Guidelines? *Journal of Business and Psychology, 16,* 457–465. doi:10.1023/a:1012881209342

Van der Heijde, C. M., & Van der Heijden, B. I. J. M. (2006). A competency based and multidimensional operationalization and measurement of employability. *Human Resource Management, 45*(3), 449–476. doi:10.1002/hrm.20119

Weathington, B. L., Bergman, S. M., & Bergman, J. Z. (2014). Training science-practitioners: Broadening the training of industrial-organizational psychologists. *Industrial and Organizational Psychology: Perspectives on Research and Practice, 7,* 35–38. doi:10.1111/iops.12101

Zelin, A. I., Oliver, J., Chau, S., Bynum, B., Carter, G., Poteet, M. L., & Doverspike, D. (2015a). Identifying the competencies, critical experiences and career paths of I-O psychologists: Industry. *The Industrial Organizational Psychologist, 53*(1), 142–151.

3

Preparing for a Career

Essential Competencies and Experiences

Sharon Glazer, Simon M. Moon, Roya Ayman, and Rita Berger

The Society for Industrial and Organizational Psychology (SIOP)'s *Guidelines for Education and Training in Industrial-Organizational Psychology* (2016) address topics and competencies that industrial-organizational (I-O) professionals and academics have deemed important. I-O knowledge, skills, and abilities (KSAs) are gained through higher education teaching methods that provide experiences inside or outside of the classroom; other KSAs are gained through employer-provided experiences. This chapter presents findings from the 2019 I-O Master's Graduate Survey (Shoenfelt, 2019a) that asked alumni of terminal master's programs about essential KSAs (aka competencies) and education-based experiences they have gained. Employers of I-O master's practitioners were invited to complete the I-O Master's Employer Survey (Shoenfelt, 2019b). Both master's alumni and their employers rated the criticality of competencies in preparing master's-level I-O practitioners for a career, indicated where the practitioner gained the KSAs (i.e., in their master's program, on the job, or through continuing education), and listed the top three competencies in terms of importance.

This chapter begins with a summary of the SIOP (2016) key competencies for graduate preparation as presented in the Graduate Survey (Shoenfelt, 2019a; see Huelsman & Shanock, 2020, for a discussion of the SIOP competencies). We include a summary of the European Network of Organizational Psychologists (ENOP) competency model to provide a possible comparison with a view toward developing curriculum for a global workforce. We then review key competencies and experiences desired by industry per a prior SIOP assessment (Zelin, Lider, & Doverspike, 2015) and findings from alumni and employers in the United States as gathered for this chapter (Shoenfelt, 2019a; Shoenfelt, 2019b). We conclude with essential competencies and experiences forecasted to become essential in our globalized world of work.

Sharon Glazer, Simon M. Moon, Roya Ayman, and Rita Berger, *Preparing for a Career* In: *Mastering the Job Market*. Edited by: Elizabeth L. Shoenfelt, Oxford University Press (2021). © Society of Industrial and Organizational Psychology. DOI: 10.1093/oso/9780190071172.003.0003

The SIOP Guidelines for Education and Training

The SIOP *Guidelines for Education and Training in Industrial-Organizational Psychology* (SIOP, 2016) present General Knowledge and Skills, Core I-O Content, and Related Areas of Competence that may be worth considering for inclusion in I-O graduate curricula. The SIOP competencies are addressed in the Graduate Survey and the Employer Survey (Shoenfelt, 2019a, 2019b), along with a subset of the specific competencies identified in the definitions of the SIOP competencies. For example, "Professional Skills" is a broad competency domain within General Knowledge and Skills and is defined as comprising a number of specific skills (SIOP, 2016). In the Graduate Survey, we included the specific skills of presentation skills, project management skills, and technical writing. Table 3.1 presents SIOP competencies and the specific competencies listed as "essential KSAs & experiences" on the Graduate Survey and the Employer Survey.

The ENOP Guidelines for Education and Training

ENOP recently updated its guidelines (i.e., reference model) for the training and education of work, organizational, and personnel (WOP) psychologists in Europe (DePolo, Peiro, & Zijlstra, 2019). The ENOP guidelines specify knowledge and skill areas (i.e., domain-specific) as well as professional and research competencies (i.e., capabilities or general knowledge and skills). In the areas of WOP psychology (WOP-P), students gain (1) an understanding of domain-specific topics (i.e., knowledge), (2) skills in assessing the situation in the work environment (i.e., diagnosing) and planning and implementing interventions to address issues identified, and (3) practice opportunities through internship, practicum, and a scholarly research project (see specific competencies and definitions at www.erasmuswop.org/competencies).

Along with these core I-O competencies, the Erasmus+ WOP program, a collaboration of several programs across universities in different European countries, articulates two additional competencies: (1) research competencies needed to set the I-O practitioner apart from related field practitioners and (2) enabling competencies that can be applied in any profession and career aspirations for effective performance. Enabling competencies include professional strategy for problem resolution and managing client relationships.

Table 3.1 Essential Competencies and Experiences Presented in the I-O Master's Graduate (Alumni) Survey Compared to SIOP Guidelines Competencies

SIOP Education & Training Guidelines (2016)	Essential Competencies & Experiences in 2019 Survey
General	
1. Ethical, legal, diversity, & international issues	• Ethics/ethical guidelines • Legal issues (e.g., EEO law, adverse impact analysis; other federal, state, local laws) • International issues (multicultural, global issues) & cross-cultural competence
2. Fields of psychology	
3. History & systems of psychology	
4. Professional skills (communication, business/research proposal development, consulting, & project management skills)	• Business acumen & consulting skills • Business/technical writing skills • Oral communication skills • Proposal development • Project management
5. Research methods	• Research methods & design • Survey development
6. Statistical methods/data analysis	• Statistical methods/data analysis (e.g., descriptive statistics & inferential statistics such as correlation, t-tests, ANOVA, regression) • Multivariate statistics (e.g., factor analysis, SEM, IRT) • Statistical software (e.g., SPSS, SAS, R, SQL)
Domain-Specific I-O Competencies	
7. Attitude theory, measurement, & change	• Attitudes, emotions, perceptions of fairness
8. Career development	• Career development
9. Criterion theory & development	• Criterion theory & development
10. Groups & teams	• Groups & teams
11. Human performance	• Human performance
12. Individual assessment	• Individual assessment
13. Individual differences	• Individual differences
14. Job evaluation & compensation	• Job evaluation & compensation
15. Job/task/work analysis/competency modeling & classification	• Job/task/work analysis/competency modeling & classification
16. Judgment & decision making	• Judgment & decision making

(Continued)

Table 3.1 Continued

SIOP Education & Training Guidelines (2016)	Essential Competencies & Experiences in 2019 Survey
17. Leadership & management	• Leadership & management
18. Occupational health & safety	• Occupational safety & health
19. Organization development	• Organization development
20. Organization theory	• Organization theory
21. Performance appraisal/management	• Performance appraisal/management
22. Personnel recruitment, selection, & placement	• Personnel recruitment, selection, & placement
23. Training: theory, delivery, program design, & evaluation	• Training (theory, delivery, program design, & evaluation)
24. Work motivation	• Work motivation
I-O Related	
25. Consumer behavior	• Consumer behavior
26. Human factors	• Human factors
	• Visual data presentation
	• Workforce planning (e.g., succession management)
	• Other

In 2016, a study of WOP-P master's alumni, including 112 respondents representing 35 countries, revealed that 79.9% reported that their studies were relevant to the work they performed (WOP-P Master's, 2019). The most important WOP-P competencies developed were assessment, design of interventions, interventions, evaluation, and communication, followed by critical thinking, self-management, problem solving, and teamwork.

Relevant Competencies and Experiences in U.S. Industries

SIOP (2019) posted information about top competencies for I-O psychologists working in consulting, academia, government, and industry based on a report of SIOP member data (Zelin, Lider, & Doverspike, 2015). In contrast to Zelin et al.'s report, which consisted of respondents who mostly held PhDs, this chapter reports findings based on alumni with a terminal master's degree. Zelin et al.'s work identified 57 competencies and experiences

Table 3.2 Top Five Competencies for Each Major Work Sector

Work Sector		
Consulting	**Government**	**Industry**
Oral communication	Integrity	Critical thinking
Ethical behavior	Ethical behavior	Oral communication
Critical thinking	Written communication	Ethical behavior
Integrity	Critical thinking	Interpersonal skills
Trustworthiness	Oral communication	Accountability

spanning up to five job levels, ranging from contributor to executive. The top five competencies within the work sectors of consulting, industry, and government are presented in Table 3.2. Three competencies surfaced in the top five regardless of the work sector: ethical behavior, critical thinking, and oral communication. Integrity and accountability also were common across all three work sectors. Table 3.3 presents the five most critical experiences within each sector.

Table 3.3 Top Five Experiences for Each Major Work Sector

Consulting	Government	Industry
"Contribute to the success of projects or consulting assignments"	"Complete highly complex projects that include a wide range of skills necessary (e.g., analytical skills, knowledge of various methodologies)"	"Execute and deliver on results"
"Develop strong relationships with client contacts"	"Deliver presentations to customers"	"Earn and maintain trust of leadership team"
"Maintain composure under pressure"	"Create and administer own projects from start to finish"	"Serve as subject matter expert"
"Present information at client meetings"	"Deliver effective briefings to senior management and/ or customers"	"Work through ambiguity and uncertainty"
"Attend client meetings to build client relationships"	"Demonstrate that project work adds value to the organization"	"Collaborate with people from different teams on various projects"

Perceptions of Essential Competencies: I-O Master's Alumni

Alumni Survey Respondents

Our chapter focuses on I-O professionals with a terminal master's degree; respondents with additional degrees in fields such as management (e.g., MBA) and/or doctoral degrees were excluded ($n = 101$). In addition, those who were not from the United States ($n = 21$), did not study in the United States ($n = 1$), did not specify the location of their university ($n = 15$), or held completely online degrees ($n = 19$) were excluded in the final analysis due to limited number of respondents. Among the 713 remaining alumni respondents, 47.1% were female, 32.7% were male, fewer than 1% were transgender, fewer than 1% indicated "prefer not to say," and 19.6% did not respond to this item. The sample's ethnicity was predominantly White (69.8%); 19.8% did not respond to this item; 2.8% were Hispanic; 2.4% were "two or more races"; 2.2% were African American; 2.2% were Asian; and 0.1% were Native American. Mean age of the participants ($n = 565$) was 34.2 ($SD = 8.5$) years, ranging from 23 to 68 years of age.

Top Competencies Identified by Alumni

Table 3.4 presents the mean criticality score for each competency as rated for current I-O alumni positions as well as where alumni learned each competency (i.e., during the I-O master's program, on the job, or through formal training or continuing education after the master's program). Table 3.5 presents the mean criticality rating by work sector, including state or local government, educational institution, nonprofit, for profit (private sector), and consulting. Competencies are presented in the same order as in Table 3.4. Across all sectors, alumni identified oral communication skills ($M = 4.70$), business acumen and consulting skills ($M = 4.27$), and project management skills ($M = 4.25$) as the top three competencies. These three competencies may best be labeled "enabling competencies." Note that respondents may be conceptualizing competencies differently than intended by the authors of the survey. For example, "leadership and management" and "judgement and decision making" are domain-specific topics studied in I-O, but as actions they also enable work performance. Thus, when respondents indicated that

Table 3.4 Alumni Ratings of the Criticality of Competencies and Where the Competencies Were Learned (Count and Valid Percentage)

Competencies	Criticality			Where Learned?				
	M	SD	n	I-O Master's Program	On the Job	Formal Training or Continuing Education[a]	n[b]	
Oral communication skills	4.70	0.57	554	255 (46.4)	238 (43.4)	9 (1.6)	549	
Business acumen & consulting skills	4.27	1.04	559	167 (30.3)	354 (64.1)	7 (1.3)	552	
Project management	4.25	0.95	555	152 (27.6)	351 (63.8)	20 (3.6)	550	
Ethics/ethical guidelines	4.05	1.16	565	298 (53.8)	195 (35.2)	10 (1.8)	554	
Leadership & management	4.05	1.17	531	232 (44.1)	250 (47.5)	14 (2.7)	526	
Business/technical writing skills	4.03	1.01	556	272 (49.7)	238 (43.5)	10 (1.8)	547	
Judgment & decision making	4.00	1.20	530	201 (38.1)	263 (49.8)	7 (1.3)	528	
Visual data presentation	3.97	1.12	557	237 (42.9)	266 (48.2)	21 (3.8)	552	
Attitudes, emotions, perceptions of fairness	3.75	1.24	554	321 (58.5)	163 (29.7)	8 (1.5)	549	
Groups & teams	3.72	1.24	553	351 (63.8)	154 (28.0)	7 (1.3)	550	
Human performance	3.63	1.32	554	370 (67.5)	110 (20.1)	5 (0.9)	548	
Career development	3.57	1.25	550	168 (30.8)	301 (55.2)	11 (2.0)	545	
Legal issues (e.g., EEO law, adverse impact analysis; other federal, state, local laws)	3.54	1.45	557	345 (63.1)	133 (24.3)	28 (5.1)	547	
Organization development	3.50	1.37	533	416 (78.5)	77 (14.5)	3 (0.6)	530	

(Continued)

Table 3.4 Continued

Competencies	Criticality			Where Learned?			n[b]
	M	SD	n	I-O Master's Program	On the Job	Formal Training or Continuing Education[a]	
Training (theory, needs analysis, design, evaluation)	3.48	1.34	532	418 (78.7)	75 (14.1)	6 (1.1)	531
Performance appraisal/management	3.48	1.36	533	386 (72.7)	111 (20.9)	5 (0.9)	531
Personnel recruitment, selection, & placement	3.45	1.47	534	369 (69.6)	125 (23.6)	3 (0.6)	530
Survey design	3.42	1.43	532	447 (84.3)	48 (9.1)	3 (0.6)	530
Work motivation	3.40	1.37	532	411 (77.8)	65 (12.3)	7 (1.3)	528
Job/task/work analysis/competency modeling & classification	3.36	1.46	531	422 (80.4)	70 (13.3)	3 (0.6)	525
Individual assessment	3.35	1.38	534	377 (71.8)	95 (18.1)	7 (1.3)	525
Individual differences	3.30	1.32	531	341 (65.1)	112 (21.4)	8 (1.5)	524
Workforce planning (e.g., succession management)	3.19	1.45	531	203 (38.7)	225 (42.9)	9 (1.7)	525
Job evaluation & compensation	3.03	1.46	533	358 (68.2)	106 (20.2)	7 (1.3)	525
Statistical methods/data analysis (e.g., descriptive statistics & inferential statistics such as correlation, t-tests, ANOVA, regression)	3.03	1.45	555	510 (92.6)	9 (1.6)	2 (0.4)	551
Proposal development	2.97	1.40	554	166 (30.4)	230 (42.1)	9 (1.6)	546
Research methods & design	2.92	1.35	555	504 (92.0)	11 (2.0)	3 (0.5)	548
Organization theory	2.80	1.35	534	432 (81.7)	19 (3.6)	3 (0.6)	529

Competency						
International issues (multicultural, global issues) & cross-cultural competence	2.64	1.34	561	160 (29.4)	215 (39.5)	15 (2.8)	544
Human factors	2.48	1.42	532	248 (47.1)	84 (16.0)	4 (0.8)	526
Statistical software (e.g., SPSS, SAS, R, SQL)	2.45	1.52	556	447 (81.0)	42 (7.6)	7 (1.3)	552
Criterion theory & development	2.26	1.30	554	411 (75.0)	16 (2.9)	3 (0.5)	548
Consumer behavior	2.23	1.39	533	121 (23.0)	130 (24.7)	8 (1.5)	526
Occupational safety & health	2.16	1.33	531	187 (35.7)	127 (24.2)	20 (3.8)	524
Multivariate statistics (e.g., factor analysis, SEM, IRT)	2.05	1.25	556	455 (82.6)	12 (2.2)	3 (0.5)	551

Note: Criticality was rated on a 5-point scale, 1 = *Not Critical* to 5 = *Extremely Critical.* Values in parentheses are the percentages of valid responses.

[a] After master's degree.

[b] The sample size for "Where learned?" includes respondents who indicated "not applicable," and some chose not to respond to the question of where the competency ought to be learned.

Table 3.5 Alumni Criticality Ratings of Surveyed Competencies by Work Sector

Survey Competencies	Work Sector				
	State/Local Government (n = 61–65)	Educational Institution (n = 30–33)	Nonprofit (n = 49–52)	For profit (n = 299–317)	Consulting (n = 67–78)
Oral communication skills	4.62 (.09)	4.50 (.13)	4.77 (.08)	4.69 (.03)	4.80 (.05)
Business acumen & consulting skills	3.75 (.17)	3.45 (.21)	3.92 (.14)	4.36 (.05)	4.83 (.05)
Project management	4.22 (.13)	4.27 (.20)	4.27 (.14)	4.19 (.05)	4.53 (.11)
Ethics/ethical guidelines	4.15 (.13)	4.18 (.17)	4.58 (.11)	3.97 (.07)	3.82 (.15)
Leadership & management	3.79 (.15)	3.94 (.22)	4.04 (.17)	4.12 (.07)	3.93 (.15)
Business/technical writing skills	4.09 (.14)	4.00 (.16)	4.06 (.15)	3.92 (.06)	4.37 (.09)
Judgment & decision making	4.10 (.16)	4.13 (.18)	3.94 (.17)	4.05 (.07)	3.65 (.16)
Visual data presentation	3.81 (.14)	3.94 (.22)	3.85 (.16)	3.99 (.06)	4.09 (.13)
Attitudes, emotions, perceptions of fairness	3.70 (.15)	3.75 (.25)	3.85 (.17)	3.76 (.07)	3.52 (.16)
Groups & teams	3.31 (.17)	3.88 (.21)	3.54 (.18)	3.81 (.07)	3.64 (.15)
Human performance	3.42 (.16)	3.28 (.24)	3.63 (.17)	3.73 (.07)	3.35 (.17)
Career development	3.10 (.17)	3.31 (.20)	3.55 (.17)	3.70 (.07)	3.42 (.16)
Legal issues (e.g., EEO law, adverse impact analysis; other federal, state, local laws)	3.91 (.17)	2.91 (.24)	3.65 (.17)	3.54 (.08)	3.34 (.17)
Organization development	3.13 (.17)	2.77 (.24)	3.46 (.18)	3.61 (.08)	3.51 (.16)
Training (theory, needs analysis, design, evaluation)	3.08 (.18)	3.16 (.26)	3.57 (.18)	3.52 (.08)	3.68 (.15)
Performance appraisal/ management	3.05 (.17)	2.87 (.26)	3.46 (.18)	3.65 (.08)	3.26 (.16)
Personnel recruitment, selection, & placement	3.79 (.18)	2.61 (.29)	3.58 (.21)	3.38 (.08)	3.62 (.16)
Survey design	3.43 (.17)	3.58 (.29)	3.66 (.20)	3.32 (.08)	3.63 (.17)

Table 3.5 Continued

Survey Competencies	Work Sector				
	State/Local Government (n = 61–65)	Educational Institution (n = 30–33)	Nonprofit (n = 49–52)	For profit (n = 299–317)	Consulting (n = 67–78)
Work motivation	2.92 (.18)	3.27 (.28)	3.24 (.19)	3.57 (.08)	3.13 (.17)
Job/task/work analysis/competency modeling & classification	3.93 (.18)	2.58 (.28)	3.34 (.20)	3.23 (.08)	3.68 (.17)
Individual assessment	3.65 (.18)	3.10 (.26)	3.22 (.19)	3.33 (.08)	3.29 (.18)
Individual differences	3.13 (.17)	3.06 (.25)	3.36 (.18)	3.36 (.08)	3.13 (.18)
Workforce planning (e.g., succession management)	2.69 (.17)	2.48 (.23)	3.04 (.21)	3.40 (.08)	2.96 (.19)
Job evaluation & compensation	2.85 (.17)	2.50 (.24)	3.06 (.22)	3.11 (.09)	3.07 (.18)
Statistical Methods/ Data Analysis (e.g., descriptive statistics & inferential statistics such as correlation, t-tests, ANOVA, regression)	3.25 (.17)	3.50 (.26)	2.92 (.21)	2.90 (.08)	3.36 (.16)
Proposal development	2.64 (.17)	2.94 (.24)	2.90 (.19)	2.88 (.08)	3.49 (.16)
Research methods & design	3.00 (.17)	3.56 (.27)	3.04 (.20)	2.84 (.08)	3.05 (.15)
Organization theory	2.65 (.18)	2.39 (.22)	2.58 (.18)	2.85 (.08)	3.01 (.16)
International issues (multicultural, global issues) & cross-cultural competence	1.83 (.12)	2.67 (.23)	2.23 (.17)	2.85 (.08)	2.69 (.16)
Human factors	2.31 (.18)	2.60 (.28)	2.18 (.19)	2.61 (.08)	2.14 (.16)
Statistical software (e.g., SPSS, SAS, R, SQL)	2.47 (.19)	2.72 (.32)	2.35 (.22)	2.38 (.09)	2.67 (.17)
Criterion theory & development	2.38 (.17)	2.13 (.22)	2.13 (.18)	2.26 (.07)	2.31 (.16)
Consumer behavior	1.53 (.12)	2.26 (.29)	2.08 (.20)	2.45 (.08)	1.96 (.15)
Occupational safety & health	1.90 (.15)	2.03 (.22)	2.24 (.20)	2.23 (.08)	1.94 (.14)
Multivariate statistics (e.g., factor analysis, SEM, IRT)	2.02 (.15)	2.25 (.25)	1.87 (.16)	2.08 (.07)	2.11 (.15)

"leadership and management" skills were developed on the job, it is clear that the competency was not interpreted as a domain-specific topic but as a general enabling competency.

Respondents in each work sector also rated oral communication as the most critical competency, and essentially the same as business acumen and consulting skills in the consulting sector. Business acumen and consulting skills, however, were not as important in the government, education, and nonprofit sectors. Across all respondents, the top three competencies among those the SIOP Guidelines (2016) identified as Core I-O Content Competencies, or I-O domain-specific competencies, were leadership and management (fifth most critical, $M = 4.05$), judgment and decision making (seventh most critical, $M = 4.00$), and attitudes, emotions, and perceptions of fairness (ninth most critical, $M = 3.75$). The top two domain-specific competencies also were the top competencies found within work sectors.

In addition to the criticality of each competency, respondents listed the three most important competencies needed to perform well in their current position.[1] The top 10 competencies (parenthetically represented as frequency or f) that emerged as most important across all alumni were project management skills ($f = 140$), communication skills ($f = 132$; specifically: oral: $f = 66$, written: $f = 9$, communication in general: $f = 57$), leadership theory and skills ($f = 127$), consulting skills ($f = 126$), data analysis ($f = 98$), personnel selection ($f = 78$), training ($f = 77$), organization development ($f = 70$), job analysis ($f = 66$), and legal issues ($f = 63$). Table 3.6 presents competencies listed by 10 or more alumni within a work sector.

Perceptions of Essential Competencies: Employers of I-O Master's-Level Professionals

Employers of I-O professionals also were asked to rate the criticality of competencies for positions filled by I-O master's-level professionals (Table 3.7). Employers located outside the United States and those who answered that they had no positions filled by I-O master's professionals were excluded; 62 employers remained in the sample. The most critical competencies identified by employers were enabling competencies: oral communication ($M = 4.82$), ethics ($M = 4.47$), business/technical writing ($M = 4.16$), and data visualization ($M = 4.16$). In terms of the SIOP Guidelines (2016) Core Competencies, or domain-specific competencies, employers identified the same top three

Table 3.6 List of Top (Write-In) Competencies by Work Sector ($f = 568$)

Work Sector				
State/Local Government	Educational Institution	Nonprofit	For Profit (Private Sector)	Consulting
Job analysis (21)	Data analysis (10)	Project management skills (18)	Consulting skills (82)	Consulting skills (21)
Personnel recruitment, selection, & placement (14)	Survey design (9)[a]	Survey design (9)	Leadership theory & skills (72)	Project management skills (19)
Consulting skills (11)			Project management skills (63)	Data analysis (16)
Data analysis (11)			Data analysis (51)	Communication skills (12)
Organization development (10)			Training (48)	Job analysis (10)
Project management skills (10)			Oral communication skills (38)	Oral communication skills (10)

[a] Competencies with 10 or more frequencies are presented except for-profit and consulting organizations, for which the top 6 competencies are presented, and for educational institution and nonprofit, for which we added the second most frequent competency (with 9 mentions).

domain-specific competencies as those identified by alumni: attitudes, emotions, and perceptions of fairness (seventh most critical, $M = 4.09$), leadership and management (eighth most critical, $M = 3.92$), and judgment and making (ninth most critical, $M = 3.92$).[2]

As did alumni, employers listed[3] the three most important competencies for successful performance in positions in their organization filled by I-O master's professionals. The 10 most frequently listed competencies were communication skills ($f = 35$, including oral [$f = 1$] and written [$f = 2$] communication skills), data analysis ($f = 22$), technical acumen ($f = 20$), interpersonal skills ($f = 18$), project management skills ($f = 13$), research skills ($f = 12$), results oriented ($f = 6$), collaboration ($f = 5$), consulting skills ($f = 5$), and attention to detail ($f = 4$).

Finally, employers were asked to indicate which competencies newly hired I-O master's employees typically develop after hire to be successful on the

Table 3.7 Employers' Ratings of the Criticality of Competencies and Where the Competencies Ought to Be Learned (Count and Valid Percentage)

Competencies	Criticality			Where Ought to Be Learned?			
	M	SD	n	I-O Master's Program	On the Job	Formal Training or Continuing Education[a]	n[b]
Oral communication skills	4.82	0.43	56	28 (54.9)	14 (27.5)	2 (3.9)	51
Ethics/ethical guidelines	4.47	0.86	58	24 (46.2)	14 (26.9)	2 (3.8)	52
Business/technical writing skills	4.16	1.02	56	29 (54.7)	17 (32.1)	1 (1.9)	53
Visual data presentation	4.16	0.98	57	33 (62.3)	17 (32.1)	0	53
Project management	4.12	0.89	57	20 (38.5)	28 (53.8)	1 (1.9)	52
Business acumen & consulting skills	4.11	1.06	57	18 (34.0)	30 (56.6)	2 (3.8)	53
Attitudes, emotions, perceptions of fairness	4.09	1.08	56	21 (40.4)	21 (40.4)	1 (1.9)	52
Leadership & management	3.92	1.09	48	20 (42.6)	21 (44.7)	4 (8.5)	47
Judgment & decision making	3.92	1.22	48	21 (44.7)	19 (40.4)	2 (4.3)	47
Job/task/work analysis/ competency modeling & classification	3.88	1.16	48	37 (80.4)	5 (10.9)	3 (6.5)	46
Legal issues (e.g., EEO law, adverse impact analysis; other federal, state, local laws)	3.77	1.25	56	27 (51.9)	12 (23.1)	7 (13.5)	52
Organization development	3.73	1.13	48	33 (70.2)	9 (19.1)	2 (4.3)	47
Work motivation	3.71	1.11	48	28 (59.6)	10 (21.3)	2 (4.3)	47
Groups & teams	3.70	1.36	56	30 (57.7)	13 (25.0)	1 (1.9)	52
Personnel recruitment, selection, & placement	3.67	1.23	48	29 (61.7)	14 (29.8)	0	47
Human performance	3.66	1.33	56	33 (63.5)	9 (17.3)	3 (5.8)	52
Research methods & design	3.65	1.13	57	46 (86.8)	2 (3.8)	2 (3.8)	53
Training (theory, needs analysis, design, evaluation)	3.63	1.16	48	36 (76.6)	8 (17.0)	0	47
Performance appraisal/ management	3.63	1.06	48	32 (68.1)	13 (27.7)	1 (2.1)	47

Table 3.7 Continued

Competencies	Criticality			Where Ought to Be Learned?			
	M	SD	n	I-O Master's Program	On the Job	Formal Training or Continuing Education[a]	n[b]
Individual assessment	3.62	1.21	47	31 (67.4)	9 (19.6)	0	46
Statistical methods/ data analysis (e.g., descriptive statistics & inferential statistics such as correlation, t-tests, ANOVA, regression)	3.60	1.27	57	49 (92.5)	2 (3.8)	0	53
Survey design	3.58	1.23	50	39 (81.3)	5 (10.4)	1 (2.1)	48
Career development	3.54	1.03	56	10 (19.6)	30 (58.8)	2 (1.8)	51
Job evaluation & compensation	3.51	1.27	47	29 (63.0)	13 (28.3)	2 (4.3)	46
Individual differences	3.51	1.12	47	32 (69.6)	9 (19.6)	0	46
Workforce planning (e.g., succession management)	3.33	1.23	48	22 (46.8)	18 (38.3)	3 (6.4)	47
Organization theory	3.17	1.26	47	39 (83.0)	3 (6.4)	1 (2.1)	47
Statistical software (e.g., SPSS, SAS, R, SQL)	3.02	1.48	57	39 (73.6)	5 (9.4)	1 (1.9)	53
Human factors	2.89	1.20	47	30 (63.8)	7 (14.9)	1 (2.1)	47
Proposal development	2.86	1.31	56	16 (30.8)	28 (53.8)	0	52
International issues (multicultural, global issues) & cross-cultural competence	2.78	1.27	58	16 (30.2)	19 (35.8)	3 (2.6)	53
Criterion theory & development	2.65	1.16	55	37 (72.5)	4 (7.8)	2 (3.9)	51
Multivariate statistics (e.g., factor analysis, SEM, IRT)	2.58	1.38	57	35 (68.6)	2 (3.9)	2 (3.9)	51
Occupational safety & health	2.27	1.18	48	12 (25.5)	15 (31.9)	7 (14.9)	47
Consumer behavior	2.19	1.30	48	18 (38.3)	9 (19.1)	2 (4.3)	47

Note: Criticality was rated on a 5-point scale, 1 = *Not Critical* to 5 = *Extremely Critical*. Values in parentheses are the percentages of the frequency in valid responses.

[a] After master's degree.

[b] The sample size for "Where learned?" includes respondents who indicated "not applicable," and some chose not to respond to the question of where the competency ought to be learned.

job. A total of 60 employers provided valid responses to the question.[4] The top 10 competencies identified that I-O master's employees typically develop after hire were business acumen (f = 21), communication (f = 11), organizational politics (f = 11), project management (f = 11), technical acumen (f = 11), presentation skills (f = 9), data analysis (f = 8), consulting (f = 8), subject (domain-specific) knowledge (f = 6), and relationship-building skills (f = 5).

Where Competencies Were and Should Be Learned

Per Table 3.4 and Table 3.7, alumni and employers both rated oral communication skills as the most critical competency. Although alumni indicated that these skills were developed just as often in their I-O master's program (46.4%) as on the job (43.4%), 54.9% of employers indicated that oral communication skills should be developed in I-O master's programs. Business acumen and consulting skills were rated as the second most critical competency by alumni and the sixth most critical by employers; 64% of I-O master's practitioners indicated these skills were developed on the job and 56.6% of employers indicated they should be developed on the job.

Alumni rated project management skills as the third most critical competency for their current job (M = 4.25), and employers rated project management skills as the fifth most critical competency for I-O master's practitioners (M = 4.12). Perhaps the most important competency learned by I-O master's graduates who complete a thesis is project management skills, as thesis students are required to conduct systematic research and are responsible for the project from start to finish (Kottke, Shultz, & Aamodt, 2020; Schneider & Mullins, 2020). The Graduate Survey (Shoenfelt, 2019a) indicated that 41.0% of alumni graduated from a program where a thesis was required and 8.6% graduated from a program where a thesis was optional; as such, 50.1% of alumni reported completing a thesis. That half of I-O master's programs do not require a thesis likely contributed to Graduate Survey respondents indicating that project management skills were primarily developed on the job (63.8%); 53.8% of employers indicated these skills should be developed on the job. Ironically, employers do not view the thesis as an important experience (M importance rating = 2.71), despite their valuing the project management skills (M criticality rating = 4.12) the thesis likely sharpens. It is quite possible that employers view an I-O master's thesis as a theoretical academic exercise and are not aware of its benefits in terms of developing project management skills.

Leadership and management skills were rated as the fifth most critical competency among alumni and the eighth most critical among employers; 44.1% of alumni learned this competency in graduate school, whereas 47.5% developed it on the job. Employers were divided in where this competency should be learned: 42.6% indicated in graduate school and 44.7% indicated on the job. Data analysis was one of the five most frequently listed responses among the top three competencies used on the job, reported by 120 alumni. Both alumni and employers reported that data analysis skills were primarily developed in an I-O master's program (92.6% and 92.5%, respectively). However, the alumni mean criticality rating for data analysis was 3.03 (SD = 1.45), thus ranking 25 out of 35 competencies; among employers the mean was 3.60 (SD = 1.27), ranking 21st most critical.

Alumni reported they learned attitudes, emotions, and perceptions of fairness in graduate school (58.5%) more so than on the job (29.7%). Employers were evenly split on where this competency should be learned (40.4% graduate school and 40.4% on the job). It is possible that employers are not familiar with the I-O psychology domain of study regarding attitudes, emotions, and perceptions of fairness. Finally, it might be noted that alumni reported very few competencies as being learned through continuing education or formal training. The competencies with the relative highest rates of learning from continuing education or training, albeit low rates in absolute terms, are visual data presentation (3.8%), occupational safety and health (3.8%), project management (3.6%), and international issues (2.8%). The only two competencies that more than five employers indicated should be learned through continuing education or formal training are occupational safety and health (14.9%) and legal issues (13.5%).

Inconsistencies between where alumni reported they developed competencies and where employers believe I-O master's professionals should develop competencies suggest that I-O graduate programs are creating unique educational experiences. Therefore, I-O students should consider what competencies and experiences programs offer that will help prepare them for their career aspirations. However, it is reassuring to know that several competencies not covered in one's graduate studies may be learned on the job.

Consistent with Zelin et al.'s (2015) career readiness report, the current assessment found that oral communication and ethics/ethical guidelines are vital competencies for an I-O career. Communication (written, oral, presentation), project management, and people management skills also may be general enabling competencies. Moreover, enabling competencies such as flexibility and adaptability, trustworthiness, integrity, interpersonal skills, accountability, oral and written communications, problem solving and critical thinking, interpersonal/social skills for teamwork (in person and virtually), innovation and creativity, continuous improvement, lifelong learning, resilience, cross-cultural competencies, specific leadership competencies, and project management are prominent in works on competencies for the I-O professional in the 21st century (Glazer, Kozusznik, & Shargo, 2012; Leuteritz, Navarro, & Berger, 2017; Ramírez Heller, Berger, & Brodbeck, 2014; Zelin et al., 2015).

Internship Experiences

Employers found value in graduates having an internship (M = 3.64, SD = 1.15). Alumni also indicated that the "internship experience prepared me for my first job" (M = 4.00, SD = 0.98 on a 5-point scale) and that the "internship helped define my career path" (M = 3.67, SD = 1.17). Although we do not have data indicating whether a practicum or internship was required or optional, 54.0% of alumni indicated that they completed a practicum and 83.6% completed an internship (see Volume 1, Chapter 4, by Kottke, Shultz, & Aamodt, 2020).

Value of the I-O Psychology Master's Degree

The perceived value of an I-O psychology master's degree was evidenced in alumni responses to two questions. On a 5-point scale, 709 alumni indicated strong agreement, with little variability, with the statement, "I have been able to apply what I learned in my master's program to the positions I have held" (M = 4.43, SD = 0.77). Second, alumni agreed that "My master's degree in I-O psychology played a substantial role in the success of my career" (M = 4.31, SD = 0.94).

Table 3.8 Alumni and Employer Perspectives on How I-O Psychology Master's Degrees Differ from Other Types of Degrees

Which of the following most differentiates those with master's degrees in I-O psychology from those with other types of degrees, but working in similar positions? (Select all that apply.)	Alumni (n = 713)	Employers (n = 143)
Familiarity with research, statistics, measurement, and how to think from a data perspective	456 (64.0%)	70 (49%)
Less likely to be persuaded by anecdotal evidence	289 (40.5%)	35 (24.5%)
More interested in the human experience of work	255 (35.8%)	36 (25.2%)
I-O psychologists use the scientist–practitioner model	255 (35.8%)	21 (14.7%)
Interventions at the individual level (e.g., satisfaction, motivation, performance improvement) rather than organizational level (e.g., profit, productivity, investment outcomes)	243 (34.1%)	28 (19.6%)
Base efforts on theoretical understanding of why people do what they do	241 (33.8%)	27 (18.9%)
I-O psychologists are psychologists; know theories of human behavior and the weight of the outcomes that can come from person-level interventions	220 (30.9%)	21 (14.7%)
More likely to conduct research	214 (30.0%)	26 (18.2%)
I-O psychologists know how to think like scientists	154 (21.6%)	30 (21%)
I-O psychologists know how to think like psychologists	185 (19.3%)	13 (9.1%)
More likely to look at performance rather than outcome	125 (17.5%)	22 (15.4%)
Focus of I-O is typically at the micro level	30 (4.2%)	5 (3.5%)

The value of I-O programs compared to human resources certificates or an MBA is the extensive training in human behavior and assessment (Gasser, Butler, Waddilove, & Tan, 2004). Indeed, in both the Graduate Survey and the Employer Survey, alumni and employers attested to the value of I-O training in developing a scientific, data-driven approach to their work when asked to identify what makes the I-O master's degree valuable in relation to other related degrees. For example, per Table 3.8, alumni (64%) and employers (49%) selected "Familiarity with research, statistics, measurement and how to think from a data perspective" more than any other option. Their I-O master's training teaches I-O practitioners to be systematic and methodical and to make data-based decisions rather than relying on hearsay, anecdotes, or subjective or biased impressions.

Forecasting Cross-Cultural Competence
as Gaining Importance

A competency that received rather low criticality ratings in the Graduate Survey is cross-cultural competence. Although few noted it as essential, the world of work is becoming more globalized and the workforce is becoming more diverse. I-O practitioners may have to work internationally or manage a global workforce, as well as work with people with ethnic, gender, and age differences, either face to face or through virtual means. The European Union demonstrated the value of cross-cultural competence when it established the Erasmus programs (European Commission Erasmus+, n.d.). The importance of cross-cultural competence is further evidenced in the 2016 Erasmus Mundus WOP-P (WOP-P Master, 2016) assessment of its alumni. WOP-P alumni indicated the most important factors their employers sought that influenced their employability included cross-cultural competencies as developed through intercultural and multicultural experiences, language capabilities, international experiences, and virtual teamwork (Erasmus Mundus Association, 2016). It is possible that the importance of cross-cultural competence is more salient in the European Erasmus program as compared to U.S. programs due to the ease of movement between countries in Europe, the more affordable cost of studies, and the greater ease of obtaining a visa to study in Europe.[5]

It is common for individuals with an international background to recognize the importance of cross-cultural competence. This type of recognition often starts in the form of a change in global identity (Glazer, Moliner, & Carmona, 2014). For example, Glazer, Berger, and Pavisic (2017) found U.S. graduate students' global identity increased significantly from before participation (Time 1) in a short-term study abroad program with peers in Spain to four weeks after their return (Time 3), whereas the global identity of their counterparts in Spain remained unchanged; it was significantly higher than the Americans at Time 1 and was equivalent to the Americans at Time 3 (which was completed four weeks after an end of study abroad [Time 2] survey). Perhaps because several students in Spain were not originally from Spain, their global identities were already high and meeting and working with U.S. students did not change that.

Currently, few I-O psychology programs in the United States prepare students for international engagements and cross-national collaborations. However, in today's workforce, students with some international experience are more competitive than those without (Glazer et al., 2014). Becoming globally minded (Holt & Seki, 2012) and cross-culturally competent in navigating administrative, political, interpersonal, and contextual factors takes time. It might take longer for people who have seldom, if ever, traveled outside their country or interacted with people from different countries. Education and experience are necessary to develop an understanding of one's own biases (Pettigrew & Tropp, 2006), to effectively work around or through them to avoid pitfalls, and to be successful across a variety of different cultural contexts. Cross-cultural or international I-O psychology presents an opportunity for preparing I-O graduates to work effectively with a nationally and culturally diverse workforce, work across national borders, and engage diplomatically and constructively with international partners in either face-to-face or computer-mediated communication.

Conclusions

Data on career-essential KSAs and competencies from the lenses of the employer and U.S. I-O master's program alumni suggest that students should look for I-O master's programs that provide opportunities to develop and practice enabling competencies (i.e., oral communication, project management, and business acumen/consulting skills), as well as ethics and technical skills in addition to domain-specific I-O knowledge. It might be noted that these same enabling competencies were identified in WOP-P master's programs (WOP-P, 2019). Although alumni and employers did not deem the Core I-O Content domain competencies as critical as enabling competencies, without domain-specific knowledge one is unlikely to have a career in I-O psychology. The enabling competencies, however, provide the I-O master's graduate with the flexibility to enter jobs in many other domains as well. The enabling competencies undoubtedly will be sharpened on the job; however, graduate programs must begin to shape these competencies as they are critical for any I-O practitioner (DePolo et al., 2019). In short, the I-O master's graduate will add value to an organization by applying domain-specific knowledge and skills gained primarily in an I-O graduate program, such as personnel psychology (e.g., job or work analysis, personnel recruitment and selection, or performance management), organizational psychology (e.g., motivation, groups, organizational theory, and organization development), and statistical analyses, vis-à-vis enabling competencies.

Notes

1. A total of 191 I-O master's program alumni responded, yielding 568 competencies specified in response to this item (191 respondents × 3 competencies, minus 5 missing). The text responses first were cleaned for capitalization and typos, and then grouped into categories by two co-authors. Then the grouping of responses was reexamined by the other two co-authors to reduce the subjectivity in the classifications. In the last stage, the second author made final adjustments to the categories.

2. Note that respondents may be conceptualizing competencies differently than intended by the authors of the survey. For example, "leadership and management" and "judgment and decision making" are domain-specific topics studied in I-O, but they also enable work performance. Thus, when respondents indicated that leadership and management are best developed on the job, it is clear that the competency was not interpreted as a domain-specific topic, but as a general enabling competency.

3. A total of 54 employers provided valid responses to the questions; therefore, there were a total of 162 responses (54 respondents × 3 competencies) to this question. The free-write text responses were analyzed using the same method described earlier for the alumni responses.

4. To avoid too many responses from any one respondent, only the first three items listed by each respondent were included in the analysis, which resulted in a total of 89 responses.

5. Note the small number (n = 21) of respondents in the Graduate Survey who indicated they did not work in the United States and only 1 of these 21 studied in Europe.

References

DePolo, M., Peiró, J. M., & Zijlstra, F. (2019). The reference model 2020. Update of the ENOP-EAWOP reference model for W&O Psychology. http://www.enop.ee/enop/pdfs/ENOP_Ref_Model.pdf

Erasmus Mundus Association. (2016). WOP-P alumni insertion into labor market survey. https://www.em-a.eu/en/home/newsdetail-ema-members-report/wop-p-alumni-insertion-into-labor-market-survey-1893.html

European Commission Erasmus+. (n.d.) The plus of Erasmus+. https://ec.europa.eu/programmes/erasmus-plus/node_en

Gasser, M., Butler, A., Waddilove, L., & Tan, R. (2004). Defining the profession of industrial-organizational psychology. *The Industrial-Organizational Psychologist, 42*(2), 15–20. https://doi.org/10.1037/e578782011-002

Glazer, S., Berger, R., & Pavisic, I. (2017, May). *Implementation of a virtually abroad program.* Paper presented at the Eastern Academy of Management, Baltimore, MD.

Glazer, S., Kozusznik, M. W., & Shargo, I. A. (2012). Global virtual teams: A cure for—or a cause of—stress In P. L. Perrewé, J. Halbesleben, & C. Rosen (Eds.), *Research in occupational stress and well being. Vol. 10: The role of the economic context on occupational stress and well being* (pp. 213–266). Bingley, UK: Emerald. https://doi.org/10.1108/S1479-3555(2012)0000010010

Glazer, S., Moliner, C., & Carmona, C. (2014). Differences in educational training models and implications from international collaborations. In R. L. Griffith, L. F. Thompson, & B. K. Armon (Eds.), *Internationalizing the curriculum in organizational psychology* (pp. 79–104). New York: Springer.

Holt, K., & Seki, K. (2012). Global leadership: A developmental shift for everyone. *Industrial and Organizational Psychology: Perspectives on Science and Practice, 5,* 196–215. https://doi.org/10.1111/j.1754-9434.2012.01431.x

Huelsman, T. J., & Shanock, L. R. (2020). The I-O master's degree curriculum: Content and modes of delivery for teaching competencies identified in SIOP's *Guidelines for Education and Training in I-O Psychology.* In E. L. Shoenfelt (Ed.), *Mastering industrial-organizational psychology: Training issues for master's level I-O psychologists* (pp. 38–56). New York: Oxford University Press.

Kottke, J. L., Shultz, K. S., & Aamodt, M. G. (2020). Importance of applied experiences: Course projects, practica, simulations, and internships. In E. L. Shoenfelt (Ed.), *Mastering industrial-organizational psychology: Training issues for master's level I-O psychologists* (pp. 57–77). New York: Oxford University Press.

Leuteritz, J.-P., Navarro, J., & Berger, R. (2017). How knowledge worker teams deal effectively with task uncertainty: The impact of transformational leadership and group development. *Frontiers in Psychology, 8,* 1339. https://doi.org/10.3389/fpsyg.2017.01339

Pettigrew, T. F., & Tropp, L. R. (2006). A meta-analytic test of intergroup contact theory. *Journal of Personality and Social Psychology, 90*(5), 751–783. https://doi.org/10.1037/0022-3514.90.5.751

Ramírez Heller, B., Berger, R., & Brodbeck F. C. (2014). Does an adequate team climate for learning predict team effectiveness and innovation potential? A psychometric validation of the team climate questionnaire for learning in an organizational context. *Procedia-Social and Behavioral Sciences, 114,* 543–550. https://doi.org/10.1016/j.sbspro.2013.12.744

Schneider, K. T., & Mullins, M. (2020). The thesis process in I-O master's programs. In E. L. Shoenfelt (Ed.), *Mastering industrial-organizational psychology: Training issues for master's level I-O psychologists*(pp. 78–95). New York: Oxford University Press.

Shoenfelt, E. L. (2019a). I-O master's graduate survey. Survey conducted for E. L. Shoenfelt (Ed.) (2021). *Mastering the job market: Career issues for master's level industrial-organizational psychologist.* New York: Oxford University Press.

Shoenfelt, E. L. (2019b). I-O master's employer survey. Survey conducted for E. L. Shoenfelt (Ed.) (2021). *Mastering the job market: Career issues for master's level industrial-organizational psychologist.* New York: Oxford University Press.

Society for Industrial and Organizational Psychology, Inc. (2016). *Guidelines for education and training in industrial-organizational psychology.* Bowling Green, OH: Author. https://www.siop.org/Portals/84/Educators/SIOP_ET_Guidelines_2017.pdf

Society for Industrial and Organizational Psychology, Inc. (2019). I-O career paths. https://www.siop.org/Careers/I-O-Career-Paths

WOP-P Master. (2019). Employability. https://www.erasmuswop.org/employability/

Zelin, A., Lider, M., & Doverspike, D. (2015, December). *SIOP career study executive report.* https://www.siop.org/Portals/84/PDFs/Professionals/SIOP_Careers_Study_Executive_Report_FINAL-Revised_031116.pdf

4

Getting a Job

What, When, Where, and How—as Well as Pitfalls to Avoid

Susan A. Walker, Lynn K. Bartels, and Comila Shahani-Denning

Industrial-organizational (I-O) psychology graduate students and recent graduates in search of their first I-O position often ask questions about the application and selection process including which jobs to apply for and how to make a good impression in the interview. To address how to get an I-O psychology position after completing an I-O psychology master's program, this chapter reviews responses from the I-O Master's Graduate Survey (Shoenfelt, 2019a), data from the I-O Master's Employer Survey (Shoenfelt, 2019b), and the experiences of three subject matter experts, each with over 30 years of I-O experience. Two of the three are tenured I-O psychology faculty members who have served as master's program directors; the third has worked in both business and consulting as an I-O psychologist and human resources (HR) manager employing I-O psychology graduates. In this chapter, career paths for I-O master's graduates, preparation for the job search while in graduate school, and the application process are discussed. Recommendations for completing the employment application, writing a résumé and cover letter, responding to a phone screen, preparing for an interview, and job offers etiquette are reviewed.

Which Career Path?

When prospective I-O graduate students are asked which career path they plan to pursue after completing their master's degree, the most common response is consulting. Reasons include anticipated glamor, high pay, travel, high-profile clients, and other perks. Students often change their minds after they learn more about the career path and better understand the pros and

Susan A. Walker, Lynn K. Bartels, and Comila Shahani-Denning, *Getting a Job* In: *Mastering the Job Market*. Edited by: Elizabeth L. Shoenfelt, Oxford University Press (2021). © Society of Industrial and Organizational Psychology. DOI: 10.1093/oso/9780190071172.003.0004 cons of working as a consultant. There are four typical career paths for I-O professionals: consulting, industry, government, and academia. Each of these paths have different requirements, and skillsets, and each can offer valuable and rewarding careers (Doverspike & Flores, 2019; Zelin, Lider, Doverspike, Oliver, & Trusty, 2014).

In the consultant route, there are two different roles. The external consulting role is more project focused with client contact, while the internal role involves internal research and development with little client contact. Although new employees may not be expected to generate business when they start, as one moves up in consulting, client facing, billable hours, sales, and client generation become and remain important if one wishes to move into partner roles (Doverspike & Flores, 2019; Zelin et al., 2015a).

For I-O master's graduates who choose to work in industry, an internal consulting role is a popular option. In this capacity, one can work as an HR specialist or a generalist. Master's graduates often work as internal consultants (e.g., organization development specialist, workforce planning analyst, HR planning specialist); their clients are the rest of the organization and their role is to proactively and/or reactively address internal organizational opportunities (Walker, 2009; Zelin et al., 2015b).

Seeking a job with the federal, state, or local government is another career option. In this career path I-O master's graduates have the opportunity to work as a specialist or an HR generalist and likely will see the value of the work they are providing to their country, state, or city. Typically, government positions tend to have job security, good benefits, and pension plans. Similar to consulting and industry jobs, there are client-facing and internal roles that might include job duties such as job analysis, job evaluation, test validation, and data analysis (Center for Organizational Research, 2015; Zelin et al., 2015d).

The final career path is academia, which is not a common path for master's graduates (Zelin, Oliver, Doverspike, Chau, Bynum, & Poteet, 2015c). Although most universities and colleges require a doctorate degree for tenure-track positions, some hire instructors to teach with a master's degree, especially if the individual has consulting or industry experience. Exploring community colleges, where many faculty have master's degrees, may be a good strategy for I-O master's graduates interested in pursuing an academic career. Teaching I-O–related courses as an adjunct faculty member while employed in consulting, industry, or government may be a viable option for those interested in teaching.

To Which Jobs Should I Apply?

When deciding which jobs to apply to, I-O master's students and graduates can start by searching job titles. The job postings on the Society for Industrial and Organizational Psychology (SIOP) I-O website's Job Network (SIOP, n.d.a), which provide a brief job summary, are an excellent starting point. Remember that organizations do not necessarily use the same job titles; read each job posting carefully. SIOP provides a sample set of I-O titles by level (SIOP, n.d.b). At the entry level, for an individual contributor with an I-O master's degree, titles include analyst, HR research specialist, project assistant, and associate consultant. As individuals progress, titles include principal/senior research scientist, principal/senior consultant, senior partner, HR director, vice president of HR, and chief HR officer. The goal for job seekers is to find jobs that align with their knowledge, skills, and abilities, and a company culture that is a good fit with their personality and interests.

How does the I-O job seeker determine which roles are appropriate for an I-O master's graduate? One of the first decisions is whether the job seeker wants to be a generalist or specialist. Generalists (e.g., HR administrator, HR manager, and employee relations advisor) are required to perform a variety of functions (e.g., policy, hiring, on-boarding, training, employee relations, safety, administration, compensation, discipline). While large organizations tend to have both generalists and specialists, a generalist is often the only HR position found in smaller companies. If the job hunter wants to be involved in a variety of HR roles, HR generalist might be the correct role. On the other hand, specialists (e.g., HRD specialist, workforce planning analyst) are typically found in larger organizations, where they might be hired for their ability to perform a specific function such as job analysis, test validation, organizational surveys, or talent development and training development. In this role, the employee may perform fewer functions but will be involved with a specific process in a specialized area with more depth (Center for Organizational Research, 2015; Walker, 2009).

In the Graduate Survey (Shoenfelt, 2019a), an overwhelming number of job titles were reported. The most common first I-O–related positions that graduates accepted after earning their master's degree were analyst, followed by specialist, manager (supervisor/manager/senior manager), and coordinator. Other titles with more than five responses included generalist, associate, and director.

Traditional I-O specialty areas were more common than generalist areas when recent graduates selected the top areas in which they currently worked. Six of the seven most common responses were traditional I-O specialist areas: data analytics (29%), talent management/leadership development (25%), consulting (24%), organization development/surveys (21%), learning and development (19%), research (14%), and psychometrics (7%). The generalist responses included employee relations (14%), recruitment/staffing (11%), HR generalist (10%), compensation (10%), operations (8%), and personnel administration (7%). The areas I-O masters' graduates were least likely to work in were health and wellness (2%), risk and safety (3%), diversity and inclusion (4%), and human resources information system (HRIS; 6%).

Elevator Pitch: Explaining I-O

Although there is a growing awareness of the field of I-O (e.g., Farnham, 2014), I-O psychologists and practitioners are still often faced with the question by employers: "What exactly is I-O psychology?" All three authors have been told numerous times that we would be welcome at an organization because their employees would benefit from therapy, indicating a definite misunderstanding of the field of I-O psychology. Clearly, I-O psychologists and practitioners need to do a better job communicating what we can do before we can expect organizations to hire us (Gasser, Whitsett, Mosley, Sullivan, Rogers, & Tan, 1998). One solution is to create an "elevator pitch," a summary that clearly communicates the value of the I-O degree in about a minute (Thoroughgood, 2010).

According to Islam (2014), a good elevator speech is compact, comprehensive, and convincing. Islam posted an elevator pitch challenge on his blog; below is a response from Elman (2014), a leadership consultant:

Just as you might go to your local doctor when you are feeling unwell, business leaders with human capital pains call on I-O Psychologists. We first listen to the organizations' HR symptoms; then we use tested scientific methods to check the organizations' pulse and finally we prescribe a course of treatments from our org-kitbag. In addition, we work closely with healthy organizations that want to avoid getting sick in the first place.

I-O master's graduates who are job hunting are encouraged to develop their own elevator pitch and to practice it until they can say it smoothly without hesitation. Job hunters may consider tailoring the speech to the organization or industry in which they are interested.

Preparing for the Job Search While in Graduate School

Preparation for the job search, and ultimately for a career, should begin while students are in graduate school. I-O graduate students should work to distinguish themselves from other applicants, including non–I-O graduates. I-O master's graduates overwhelmingly reported that including applied I-O projects as part of coursework (62%) was most useful in preparing for their careers. Participating in I-O projects in organizations outside of classwork (37%) and completing internships (31%) also were considered useful in preparing for careers (Shoenfelt, 2019a). Graduate students should leverage these applied experiences by including them in their online profiles, applications, résumés, cover letters, and interview responses.

I-O master's graduates who need (or want) to supplement their experience are encouraged to contact local nonprofit organizations to volunteer time (e.g., performing a job analysis, standardizing interview materials, creating an on-boarding orientation for volunteers). One recent graduate built a performance management system for her synagogue. Another graduate created a new hire orientation program for a nonprofit organization's volunteers. Yet another assisted Goodwill in creating an employee database. In addition to gaining hands-on experience and assisting an organization with a need, these pro bono experiences provide networking opportunities and should be included on the résumé and leveraged during the job search (Shoenfelt et al., 2015; Shoenfelt, Hill-Fotouhi, Kedenburg, Palmer, Seibert, & Walker, 2017; Walker, 2009).

While in graduate school, I-O master's students should begin to create a professional image. This is the time to update LinkedIn profiles, remove anything questionable from social media sites (or restrict access through site security settings), and even begin shopping for appropriate interview attire. Zide, Elman, and Shahani-Denning (2014) suggested that I-O practitioners can optimize their LinkedIn profiles by updating all relevant experiences, education, and certifications and including keywords that may appear in searches. I-O master's students should conduct an internet search on their name both on browsers and social media sites to preview what a potential employer might see. If someone online shares the same name as you do, you may consider adding a middle name or initial to your résumé/profile so that the right person shows up when an employer conducts an online search (Shoenfelt et al., 2017; Zide et al., 2014).

In the Employer Survey (Shoenfelt, 2019b), employers were asked to select the characteristics that differentiate an average applicant from a superior applicant. Two types of skills were examined: hard skills related to business and technical competencies and soft skills, which are personal characteristics that facilitate working well with others (Robles, 2012). The hard skills that employers of I-O master's graduates identified as differentiating average from superior applicants included business savvy/acumen, (47.4%), technical knowledge (46.5%), experience (45.6%), research skills (29.8%), and knowledge of your business (28.1%). Soft skills included communication skills (77.2%), attitude (76.3%), work ethic (69.3%), and interpersonal skills (63.2%). Clearly, soft skills were identified more often by employers when differentiating job applicants. I-O master's students should be aware of the importance of soft skills and seek opportunities to practice, receive feedback on, and develop their soft skills throughout their graduate program, including during internships and consulting projects. They should ensure that their job search materials (e.g., résumé, cover letter, online profiles) and interactions (e.g., elevator speech, interview responses) positively portray their interpersonal skills. Graduate programs can and should focus on helping graduate students develop soft skills through activities such as team projects, presentations, work opportunities, and assessment centers (Kottke, Schultz, & Aamodt, 2020, Shoenfelt et al., 2015).

Although they weren't identified as frequently as differentiating between average and superior applicants, hard skills are important and often are assessed during the selection process (Doverspike & Flores, 2019). Technical skills can be developed through coursework, research, and work experiences. I-O master's graduates should be prepared to appropriately respond to interview questions and assessments designed to measure their technical skills (Shoenfelt et al., 2015, 2017).

Master's I-O employers were asked to rate (on a scale from 1 = not important to 5 = very important) how important certain experiences were when hiring master's-level I-O applicants (Shoenfelt, 2019b). Not surprisingly, employers rated work-related experiences as more important than academic experiences. The majority of employers (68%) rated completing an internship as important, while only 32% of employers rated completing a thesis as important. Most employers (60%) didn't care whether the internship was paid or whether the applicant's degree was from an online program. Employers (50%) indicated that references from the internship employer were more important than references from the graduate program (41%). When asked whether any professional certifications were required or preferred, 94% of employers indicated they were neither required nor preferred. The only certifications mentioned by multiple employers were the Society for Human Resource Management (SHRM)'s Certified Professional or Senior Certified Professional.

I-O faculty and internship supervisors can support graduate students in their job search efforts by providing feedback on résumés, cover letters, elevator speeches, and interview responses. Students should share with faculty and internship supervisors their job search focus as these advisors may be able to share job leads and provide references or confirm duties. Working with faculty members and internship supervisors may help I-O master's graduates leverage others' networking contacts and industry knowledge. In addition, I-O students should use the resources available through their university career development centers.

The Job Search

The application and selection process is an exciting (and somewhat nerve-racking) opportunity for the job seeker to learn about prospective employers and their organizations and to evaluate fit, including working hours, travel, duties, hiring manager, colleagues, culture, and environment. The I-O selection process tends to be a multistep procedure that can take three to six months from posting the position to the start date (Shoenfelt, Kottke, Stone, Agarwal, Seibert, & Walker, 2009; Walker, 2009).

Networking, internships (paid or unpaid), and soft skills were identified as key factors for most I-O master's graduates in finding their first I-O job (Shoenfelt, 2019a). When asked how many jobs students applied to before receiving their first I-O-related offer, the median number was between four and five jobs. Eighty percent of respondents reported finding a job within six months after graduation.

To begin the job search, job seekers are encouraged to research organizations before applying and interviewing. Online sources like Glassdoor are easy to use and provide valuable organizational information. Potential applicants are encouraged to access organizational websites, check stock prices, review recent news coverage, and consider how they can add value to the organizations. Job seekers should be prepared for hiring organizations to research their online presence; therefore, ensure it is professional, accurate, and positive.

Application Materials: Application, Résumé, and Cover Letter

When applying for each position, expect to complete an application and submit a résumé and cover letter. Candidates may be asked to submit their LinkedIn profile. Henceforth in this chapter, these submitted materials will be referred to as the "application materials."

Many, if not most, medium to large employers use applicant tracking systems (ATS) to post positions and allow applicants to search and apply for open positions. ATS enable companies to collect, screen, and process large numbers of applicants. Some ATS allow employers to search for candidates with specific knowledge, skills, and abilities (KSAs), education, and/or credentials. ATS may enable hiring managers/recruiters to search for keywords or phrases in the submitted materials. These systems often allow prescreen questions that typically ask whether the applicant meets (and/or exceeds) the required minimum qualifications for the position. Some ATS calculate a score for each candidate. Typically, these systems operate on a first in/first out premise. ATS often allow hiring managers/recruiters to sort applicants by score, application date, or both. In addition, particular company policies may require that the hiring manager/recruiter review only a limited number of applicants and/or allow access to additional applicants only after elimination of a certain number of applicants. ATS may be programmed to automatically close a job posting when a predetermined number of candidates (or applicants) apply or after a predefined date (Shoenfelt et al., 2017).

What are the implications of ATS for the I-O master's applicant? Given that I-O–related postings may draw hundreds of applicants, if you see a posting that interests you and for which you are qualified, apply immediately. Do not wait, or the posting may not be available. With job postings readily available on the internet, postings tend to attract high numbers of candidates; competition for a position can be fierce.

One frequently asked question is "Must I meet all of the 'qualifications' requested?" The answer is a definite "maybe." Typically, if a qualification is listed, it is required and often companies will screen out candidates who do not possess these requirements. The key word is "often." Other qualifications may be listed as "preferred" (or "desirable"). Sometimes candidates do not apply for a position when they don't possess qualifications listed as "preferred" (i.e., they are not required). Accordingly, some recruiters suggest graduates should not be discouraged if they do not meet all the listed qualifications. A candidate who is passionate about a position and meets most of the qualifications should still apply.

Another question job seekers often ask is what they can do to increase their chances of success. It is important for applicants to carefully read the job posting, especially the minimum qualifications section, and, where appropriate, to align their application materials to demonstrate fit to the position. This does not mean you should change your experience or the duties you actually performed; making such changes would amount to falsification, which could get you eliminated as an applicant or terminated later as an employee. In most jobs, employees perform 5 to 12 duties, but on most résumés, applicants tend to highlight only a few of these duties. If you have experience performing the duties required and/or preferred by the job posting, it should be evident in the application materials you submit (Shoenfelt et al., 2017). In addition, phrases used in the job description should also be present in your application materials. If you have conducted employee training and the job description lists "experience in delivering learning and development to team members," incorporate the terms "learning and development" and "team members" into your application (Walker, 2009). Although customization such as this may be time consuming, it can be very effective and provides another opportunity for you to highlight where you stand out.

Also, job seekers should follow ATS/application directions carefully to ensure that their application is not flagged or turned down for incomplete or contradictory information. Most applications specify something such as *In this section, please document all positions you have held during the last 10 years. Do not leave any gaps.* If you are 24 years old, this might appear to be impossible because you likely have not been employed for 10 years. In this situation, applicants are encouraged to list, for example, "high school student/ not employed" and specify the dates. Ensure that dates on all application materials are accurate and consistent (Shoenfelt et al., 2017; Walker, 2009).

ATS Prescreen Questions

Prescreen questions typically are incorporated into ATS; either they are part of the application or are sent to potential applicants before or after application completion. Prescreen questions determine whether those who apply meet the minimum qualifications for the position and, thereby, truly are applicants. For example, a prescreen question might be *How many years of experience do you have in human resources?* If the position requires two years of HR experience, all candidates who apply and answer that they have less than two years of HR experience will be eliminated from further consideration for this position.

One of the most frequent reasons candidates are not considered past this initial selection step is their responses to ATS prescreen questions. Unfortunately, some who apply will be qualified but will not read the questions carefully and will be eliminated from future consideration—for example, responding "no" to *Are you legally authorized to work in the United States for any employer?* when the applicant actually is authorized. Another potential error is when a position requires a "master's degree in industrial-organizational psychology" and a student who is soon to graduate answers "no." If you will possess the degree by the hire date or in the next 90 days, respond "yes." Note that employers may ask for a transcript confirming the completion of the applicant's degree (Shoenfelt et al., 2017; Walker, 2009).

Application, Résumé, and Cover Letter Do's

Job seekers are encouraged to follow these recommendations (Shoenfelt et al., 2015, 2017; Walker, 2009):

1. Do have an email address that is professional. Email addresses and social media sites including nonprofessional terms, meanings, or photos are not appropriate (e.g., beerdrinker, dizzygirl, party_guy, or photos of you drunk at a professional association party).
2. Do proofread. Spelling, grammatical, and formatting errors may be perceived as a lack of attention to detail. Referring to the company by the wrong name and stating interest in the wrong position title are common errors. For example, it's easy to update a cover letter you wrote for another company but fail to change the company name.

3. Do keep it short and the format clean. Applicants who have recently completed a master's degree should limit both their cover letter and résumé to one page in length.

4. Do clearly name any file submitted in the application process, such as John Smith Resume 2-1-2020.pdf. Typically, systems require pdf files be submitted, but read the submission directions carefully to determine the appropriate file format or file name.

5. Do highlight your strengths, but be accurate. Inaccurate or exaggerated job titles, dates, duties, coursework, and degree title can be grounds for termination even if they are discovered years later. For example, don't claim you "led" a validation project if you didn't join the project until three months after it began.

6. Do be prepared to discuss every statement on your résumé.

7. Do ensure consistency between your résumé, cover letter, application, and LinkedIn profile. What will recruiters think when they see five jobs listed on your résumé but only three on your application? And, to make it worse, what if one of the three jobs listed has a different job title on the application than the résumé? If you have a lot of non–I-O experience, one suggestion is to list all jobs on your application but on your résumé have an "I-O–Related Experience" section and an "Other Job Experience" section and then list jobs in the appropriate section.

8. Do make it clear in your cover letter and/or résumé that you meet (or exceed) the minimum requirements for this position.

9. Do ask people for permission before you list them as references. Provide your references with a current copy of your résumé.

10. Do keep a log of every position to which you have applied. Note the company name, position, where you have saved a copy of the job posting, and any contact names.

Phone Screens

Phone screens are often another hurdle in a multiple-hurdle selection process. Phone screens occur when a hiring manager/recruiter, or even a potential colleague, calls an applicant after the applicant has submitted an application but prior to a request for a face-to-face or virtual interview. Employers are evaluating both your soft and technical skills during this step. The phone screen is a step many applicants fail to take seriously—but then they are surprised when they do not move to the next step in the selection process. Here are some tips for a successful phone screen (Shoenfelt et al., 2017; Walker, 2009).

1. If you are in the process of applying to jobs, always answer the phone professionally, have a professional message on your voicemail, and check your messages daily. Answering the phone with "yeah" or having a voicemail message that says "we are out partying" is not wise.

2. When you get a call from a potential employer, stop what you are doing, note the name and title of who is calling, and listen. If you are in the middle of playing Frisbee with your dog, politely ask if you can call back when you can give your full attention to the call (preferably within 24 hours) and suggest options for the callback date/time. Telling the recruiter that you are too busy (e.g., exams, thesis) and not available for two weeks is not recommended.

3. Check and update your application log. Do not be the applicant who says, "I don't remember applying to your organization." Update your application log with the name and title of the caller.

4. Realize that you may be 1 of 30 people being phone screened or even 1 of 100 (or more). Do not stop job hunting; continue your search until you have accepted a written offer.

5. Answer the questions asked in the phone screen honestly and succinctly. Don't take over the call. Don't interrogate the caller about his or her background or inquire about compensation.

6. It is acceptable to ask about the next step in the hiring process and the timeline for filling the position. However, don't be disappointed if few details are provided.

7. Thank the caller for the call. The Employer Survey (Shoenfelt, 2019b) indicated that soft skills, including communications, attitude, and positivity, were mentioned as critical more often than technical skills in differentiating between average and excellent employees. Soft skills may be assessed in the phone screen.

Assessments

Another potential step in a multiple-hurdle selection process is assessments, including work samples, role playing, examination of data, or drafting project plans (Walker, 2009). Assessments may include cognitive ability and personality assessments. Assessments may be administered via computer or pen and paper and may be completed onsite or offsite. Consulting firms, especially ones that have a testing/assessment business line, often require applicants to complete assessments (Doverspike & Flores, 2019). Depending on the corporation or government agency and the level of the position, some form of assessment should be expected.

Treat assessments as an actual work assignment. Read the instructions carefully. Note time allowed, file-naming conventions, procedure for submitting, and whom to contact if there are questions or technical problems. Don't expect to receive feedback on your submission. If feedback is provided, listen, take notes, and thank the person sharing the information (even if you disagree). Remember that, formally or informally, your response to the feedback may impact the selection outcome. Arguing with the employer providing feedback is not a good response and may lead to an undesirable outcome—that is, you will not be hired (Walker, 2009).

Interviews

Today, the formats of interviews may vary greatly. Based on one author's experience including volunteer work with job seekers, interviews are changing rapidly. Although interviews are still typically done in person, virtual interviews such as via Skype or FaceTime have become popular due to the ease of administration and the savings in travel costs and time. Typically interviews are conducted one on one or an applicant is interviewed by a panel of three to five stakeholders, managers, and/or HR team members. Recently, one-way video recorded interviews have been implemented with applicants, being videotaped responding to each question. Some systems allow applicants to take breaks from recording, watch their responses, and re-record them, if desired. A one-way video interview allows the hiring manager or team members to review each submission at their convenience.

Interview questions may include behavior-based and/or technical questions (Shoenfelt et al., 2015, 2017; Walker, 2009). Examples of behavior-based questions are:

- Tell me about a time you had to work with a difficult coworker.
- Tell me about a time you missed a deadline.
- Tell me about a time you encountered obstacles in completing a project.

Examples of technical questions include:

- How is a VLOOKUP used in Excel?
- List the steps you would take to develop a content-valid selection process for hiring front-line managers.
- You have developed a test that has adverse impact. How would you explain the situation to the legal department at your company? What would be your recommendations to executive leadership at your company?

How to Prepare for the Interview

The average corporate job posting gets 250 applications, but typically only four to six applicants are interviewed and only one is hired (Economy, 2015). One recent I-O graduate withdrew from an internship selection process because she had eight interviews for full-time positions. Three months later, after being turned down for all eight, she reapplied for the internship (Shoenfelt et al., 2017).

On the Graduate Survey (Shoenfelt, 2019a), I-O master's graduates were asked what they did to prepare for the interview(s) that helped them land their first I-O–related position. Many graduates practiced alone (61.4%) rather than practicing with family and friends (28.1%), with faculty (7.3%), or with their university career center (6.7%). Although practicing alone may be an important first step in preparing for an interview, feedback from others may help you identify interviewing mistakes that were not readily apparent or ways you can improve your interview responses. When asked to identify the one action that was most helpful in preparing for interviews for their first I-O psychology–related position, the most commonly selected responses were "reviewed my own résumé" (71.6%) and "reviewed job posting or job description" (71.6%). Although these are critical steps, there are many additional things you can do to prepare for a job interview.

Here are some tips for interview preparation:

1. Ask questions and listen when contacted about the interview. Note the date, time, and location of the interview. We recommend asking about interview format, number of interviewers, interviewers' titles, and interview length. "Is there anything I need to bring to the interview?" is a good follow-up question.

2. Make a two-column chart. In the first column, cut and paste from the posting or job description the minimum required and preferred qualifications for the position. In the second column, list how you meet or exceed these qualifications. Cut and paste the second column from your résumé and note specific examples of how each qualification is met or exceeded (Walker, 2009).

3. Use the STAR (Situation—Task—Action—Results) technique to organize your responses to behavior-based interview questions and practice providing responses in the STAR format. Aim for responses that are complete but take less than two minutes, as illustrated in the following example.

> Situation: In graduate school, while working on a survey consulting project for my thesis chair . . .
>
> Task: I was partnered to work on the project with a person who was known as a very critical person who rarely socialized.
>
> Action: After I carefully reviewed the project scope and timeline, I knew that neither of us could accomplish the project alone. I asked my project partner to meet me for a cup of coffee. In the informal setting, I asked her about her concerns with the project and how she would address them. When I really listened to her, I learned we had similar concerns but different and complementary skills.
>
> Result: By taking the time and effort to meet and listen to each other, we were able to proactively address some potential issues with the project. We finished two days ahead of schedule and produced a better work product than either of us could have alone. Our professor was very pleased with the results. The coworker and I went on to successfully complete several more projects together.

4. Anticipate technical questions and outline answers ahead of time. Study for the interview. For example, if you took statistics and psychometrics your first year of graduate school and the job focuses on this area, study your notes and old textbooks to prepare for the interview (Shoenfelt, Walker, Walker, Maue, & Snyder, 2007).

5. Ask your professors for advice regarding interviewing. Ask your professors and classmates to provide feedback on your strengths and weaknesses.

6. Record yourself answering interview questions, listen to the recording, identify where you can improve your response(s), and practice the revised response(s).

7. Promote your strengths, but be honest.

8. Respect any confidentiality agreements you have previously made. An interviewer would rather hear a general description regarding a project than have an applicant violate confidentiality. Any applicant who is willing to share confidential information about the work done in a previous position or internship cannot be trusted not to do the same in the future (Shoenfelt et al., 2015).

9. Do NOT stop job hunting! Too often new graduates assume that if they have an interview (or multiple interviews), they will get an offer, so they stop job hunting. Continue your job search until you have accepted a job offer (Shoenfelt et al., 2017).

Dos & Don'ts During the Interview

Here are critical actions to take during the interview (Shoenfelt et al., 2017; Walker, 2009):

1. Do be prepared to sell/explain why you meet (or exceed) the position minimum requirements.

2. Do get to the interview location 15 minutes before the interview. Take into consideration weather, traffic, parking, etc. to ensure you arrive early to the interview.

3. Do prepare informed questions to ask about the position and organization. These questions should demonstrate that you are putting yourself in the role of the job holder.

4. Do say, "I don't know, but I would like to learn more" if you don't know an answer. Don't make up an answer or bluff.

5. Do practice logging on and interviewing with Skype, Zoom, FaceTime, etc. prior to a virtual interview. Ensure there will be no interruptions and that the background (what is behind you on screen) is professional.

6. Do be prepared to answer "Why are you the best candidate?" and/or "Are there any other job-related KSAs that we have not asked about that we should know?"

7. Don't badmouth others, including current or former companies, bosses, coworkers, or professors. I-O is a well-connected discipline

and there may be just a few degrees of separation between your interviewer and your associates.

8. Don't use the same example/project for every question. Identify a variety of examples and review your role in each project prior to the interview.

9. Don't respond that you NEVER made a mistake or NEVER had a conflict with others. It will hurt your credibility.

10. Don't be a victim of self-imposed detractors (inappropriate language, smacking or chewing gum, playing with your hair, failing to sit up straight in the chair, etc.). These actions are unprofessional and detract from your professional appearance.

11. Don't be a wardrobe malfunction. It is better to be overdressed than underdressed. A safe bet is a dark or neutral-colored suit with a white, cream, or blue dress shirt. Cleavage, heavy makeup, sports shoes, and tight or ill-fitting clothing can be detractors.

12. Don't forget to send a thank-you email or note after the interview. It is good business etiquette and represents another opportunity to remind the interviewer of who you are.

Applicant Frustrations

The application and selection process can appear to the job hunter to move in slow motion. There are several reasons why the job search at this level typically takes three to six months. First, the internet has increased the average number of applicants. A typical corporate job posting yields many applicants (Economy, 2015). Second, hiring managers in I-O departments often have limited support and large spans of control. The manager often is both a leader and a specialist who is on a deadline for work products. Thus, when there's a position opening, managers have to choose between doing required work and filling the position. Finally, thorough selection processes administered appropriately with large numbers of applicants tend to be time consuming.

Typically applicants will receive no or very little feedback (e.g., a letter thanking them for applying but stating that a more qualified applicant was selected) from the selection process. However, some hiring managers will provide intern applicants that make it to an interview with limited feedback, if requested.

Job Offers

Successful applicants are offered a job. Typically, initial offers are made verbally, followed up with a written offer letter. Signing and returning the offer letter indicates that the applicant accepts the job under the conditions detailed (e.g., work location, work schedule, benefits, salary, bonus). NOTE: Offer letters typically are not employment contracts or employment agreements. If you have questions, consult an attorney.

What if you get a better offer after you've accepted/signed a job offer or started a job? This is a difficult situation and may not have a clear answer. Thirty years ago, the response would most likely have been that you signed an offer, made a commitment, and need to abide by that commitment. Now, the answer is not completely clear.

Acceptable reasons for backing out of a signed offer for another offer may include higher pay, better benefits, better culture fit, shorter commute, and the belief that the company would back out of an offer if needed (Doyle, 2019; Share, n.d.). After reviewing the offer letter to ensure there are no legal implications, Boogaard (n.d.) suggested three additional steps in declining an accepted job offer:

1. Show appreciation to the company that provided the initial offer by advising them of your decision and thanking them for their time and interest.
2. Explain your situation and reasons for taking the new offer.
3. Realize that there are consequences. Boogaard concluded, "Rejecting a job offer you had already accepted is likely to [negatively] impact your professional reputation." You have likely burned your reputation with the company, hiring manager, HR, and anyone on the selection team (Boogaard, n.d.; Emily Post Institute, 2019). Finally, your faculty reference may not view the change favorably, especially if the professor leveraged a contact to support you.

The preferred strategy and the strategy we recommend is to be proactive. When you receive an offer, immediately contact the hiring manager at other organizations where you have interviewed, reiterate your interest, advise them that you have an offer from another employer, inquire about the potential of a forthcoming offer from their organization, and thank them for their time and interest (Doyle, 2019). This process is not only professional and polite but may get you another offer prior to signing the first offer and preclude the unfortunate situation described earlier.

Conclusions

The job search and selection process can be detailed, time consuming, and stressful. However, with some planning and preparation while you are in graduate school and during the selection and hiring process, the job search can be more manageable and successful. By putting as much effort into the process as you do in your graduate classes and taking advantage of resources such as I-O faculty and university career centers, you maximize your chances for a successful job search, typically landing a job in six months or sooner.

References

Boogaard, K. (n.d.). Can you decline a job offer after you've accepted it. https://www.ziprecruiter.com/blog/can-you-decline-a-job-offer-after-youve-accepted-it/

Center for Organizational Research. (2015, December). SIOP career study executive report. https://www.siop.org/Careers/I-O-Career-Paths

Doverspike, D., & Flores, C. (2019). *Becoming an industrial-organizational psychologist.* 1st ed. New York: Routledge. https://doi.org/10.4324/9781351061865

Doyle, A. (2019). How to decline a job offer you already accepted. https://www.thebalancecareers.com/how-to-turn-down-a-job-offer-you-already-accepted-2061404

Economy, P. (2015). 11 interesting hiring statistics you should know. https://www.inc.com/peter-economy/19-interesting-hiring-statistics-you-should-know.html

Elman, B. (2014). Re: Contest: Your elevator pitch [blog comment]. https://psychologyofwork.wordpress.com/2014/01/30/contest-your-elevator-pitch/

Emily Post Institute, Inc. (2019) Backing out of an accepted job offer. https://emilypost.com/advice/backing-out-on-an-accepted-job-offer/

Farnham, A. (2014). 20 fastest-growing occupations. https://abcnews.go.com/Business/americas-20-fastest-growing-jobs-surprise/story?id=22364716

Gasser, M., Whitsett, D., Mosley, N., Sullivan, K., Rogers, T., & Tan, R. (1998). I-O psychology: What's your line? *The Industrial-Organizational Psychologist, 35*(4), 120–126. https://doi.org/10.1037/e577062011-013

Kottke, J. L., Shultz, K. S., & Aamodt, M. G. (2020). Importance of applied experiences: Course projects, practica, simulations, and internships. In E. L. Shoenfelt (Ed.), *Mastering industrial-organizational psychology: Training issues for master's level I-O psychologists* (pp. 57–77). New York: Oxford University Press.

Islam, S. (2014) Contest: Your elevator pitch. https://psychologyofwork.wordpress.com/2014/01/30/contest-your-elevator-pitch/

Robles, M. M. (2012). Executive perceptions of the top 10 soft skills needed in today's workplace. *Business Communication Quarterly*, *75*(4), 453–465. https://doi.org/10.1177/1080569912460400

Share, J. (n.d.). Five tips for how to back out of a job. https://www.livecareer.com/resources/jobs/offers/how-to-back-out-of-an-accepted

Shoenfelt, E. L. (2019a). I-O master's graduate survey. Survey conducted for E. L. Shoenfelt (Ed.) (2021). *Mastering the job market: Career issues for master's level industrial-organizational psychologist*. New York: Oxford University Press.

Shoenfelt, E. L. (2019b). I-O master's employer survey. Survey conducted for E. L. Shoenfelt (Ed.) (2021). *Mastering the job market: Career issues for master's level industrial-organizational psychologist*. New York: Oxford University Press.

Shoenfelt, E. L., Hill-Fotouhi, C. H., Kedenburg, G. L., Palmer, L., Seibert, J., & Walker, S. A. (2017, April). "Mastering" the job market: Advice from master's level professionals. Presented at the Annual Conference of the Society for Industrial & Organizational Psychology, Orlando, FL.

Shoenfelt, E. L., Kottke, J. L., Stone, N. J., Agarwal, S., Seibert, J., & Walker, S. A. (2009, April). I/O master's careers: Landing the job. Presented at the 24th Annual Conference of the Society for Industrial-Organizational Psychology, New Orleans, LA. https://doi.org/10.1037/e518422013-859

Shoenfelt, E. L., Kottke, J. L., Stone, N. J., Dolen, M., Hill-Fotouhi, C., Seibert, J., & Walker, S. A. (2015, April). What employers want in master's hires: Landing the first job. Presented at the Annual Conference of the Society for Industrial and Organizational Psychology, Philadelphia, PA.

Shoenfelt, E. L., Walker, S. A., Walker, A. G., Maue, A. E., & Snyder, L. (2007, April). I/O master's careers: Successful paths to divergent destinations. Presented at the 2007 Annual Conference of the Society for Industrial and Organizational Psychology, New York, NY.

SIOP. (n.d.a) I/O job network. https://www.siop.org/Careers/Job-Search

SIOP. (n.d.b) Common job titles across sectors. https://www.siop.org/Careers/I-O-Career-Paths/Common-Job-Title

Thoroughgood, C. (2010). The two-minute elevator speech: Communicating value and expertise as I-O psychologists to everyone else. *The Industrial-Organizational Psychologist*, *48*(1), 121–126. https://doi.org/10.1037/e579012011-017

Walker, S. A. (2009, April). Master's Consortium nominated speaker at the 24th Annual Conference of the Society of Industrial and Organizational Psychology. New Orleans, LA.

Zelin, A. I., Lider, M., Doverspike, D., Oliver, J., & Trusty, M. (2014). Competencies and experiences critical for entry-level success for I-O psychologists. *Industrial and Organizational Psychology: Perspectives in Science and Practice*, *7*, 65–71. https://doi.org/10.1111/iops.12108

Zelin, A. I., Oliver, J., Chau, S., Bynum, B., Carter, G., Poteet, M. L., & Doverspike, D. (2015a, April). Identifying the competencies, critical experiences, and career paths of I-O psychologists: Consulting. *The Industrial-Organizational Psychologist*, *52*(4), 122–130. http://www.siop.org/tip/april15/PDF/zelin.pdf

Zelin, A. I., Oliver, J., Chau, S., Bynum, B., Carter, G., Poteet, M. L., & Doverspike, D. (2015b, July). Identifying the competencies, critical experiences, and career paths of I-O psychologists: Industry. *The Industrial-Organizational Psychologist*, *53*(1), 142–151. https://pdfs.semanticscholar.org/f57a/a59f2a59cca0d694d68b2d36ba91017bf570.pdf

Zelin, A. I., Oliver, J., Doverspike, D., Chau, S., Bynum, B., & Poteet, M. L. (2015c, January). Identifying competencies, critical experiences, and career paths of I-O psychologists: Academia. *The Industrial-Organizational Psychologist, 52*(3), 149–157. http://www.siop.org/tip/jan15/pdf/zelin.pdf

Zelin, A. I., Oliver, J., Chau, S., Bynum, B., Carter, G., Poteet, M. L., & Doverspike, D. (2015d, October). Identifying the competencies, critical experiences, and career paths of I-O psychologists: Government. *The Industrial-Organizational Psychologist, 53*(2), 118–127.

Zide, J., Elman, B., & Shahani-Denning, C. (2014). LinkedIn and recruitment: How profiles differ across occupations. *Employee Relations, 36*, 583–604. https://doi.org/10.1108/ER-07-2013-0086

5

Riding the Rails as an Industrial-Organizational Psychology Master's Professional

On-boarding and Off-boarding

Christopher J. L. Cunningham and Nora P. Reilly

Hey, Chris!
Just dropping you a line to let you know how life is on the other side of graduation. It seemed like it would be such a long trip when we were in the program together, but this train is moving sooo fast now. I got a job! A good one! It was incredible how much help our alumni network was in landing it; it really didn't take that long (right at 3 months) and I had a few choices because of my I-O master's degree. So far, I've been to orientation and was surprised. The company gave a group of us from all different levels in the org a two-day overview, mostly filling out paperwork, accessing the computer and learning policies. Nothing special about my job was covered. Seems like I'll need to find out more about how this place really works on my own. I guess I'll be searching for my own mentor soon and setting up meetings with other folks to learn more. This week I've got coffee and lunch plans with three more senior associates. Hopefully these meetings will help me avoid feeling like a stranger, but I guess my psychological contract is still intact. ☺Though I'm not settled in yet, you know me: I plan to ask a lot of questions. I doubt I'll stay here forever (shhhhh...they know that, right?), but at least I got a seat on this wild ride.

I'll keep in touch, Nora

Most industrial-organizational (I-O) psychology master's graduates can expect to hold a number of different jobs over the course of their career. In this chapter, we discuss the important activities of on-boarding and off-boarding; that is, the activities organizations undertake to ensure their employees have smooth transitions into and out of jobs, respectively. As new I-O master's

Christopher J. L. Cunningham and Nora P. Reilly, *Riding the Rails as an Industrial-Organizational Psychology Master's Professional* In: *Mastering the Job Market*. Edited by: Elizabeth L. Shoenfelt, Oxford University Press (2021). © Society of Industrial and Organizational Psychology. DOI: 10.1093/oso/9780190071172.003.0005 graduates embark on the first job of their career, whether in consulting, industry, or government, they have the journey of a lifetime ahead as they pursue career objectives and manage career transitions. We employ the metaphor of a journey by train to present considerations and insights into navigating these transitions.

Preparing for the Journey

We each have a number of possible futures; the postcard above presents an example of one short segment of an I-O master's graduate's path forward. Whether we hear updates in a postcard, email, or LinkedIn notification, the message is much the same. In the mind of most I-O master's students, the route to career success begins with earning a master's degree in I-O psychology. An I-O master's degree is a good place to begin the journey, especially if the master's program curriculum is aligned with the Society for Industrial and Organizational Psychology's (SIOP) *Guidelines for Education and Training in Industrial-Organizational Psychology* (SIOP, 2016), which are designed to ensure graduates of I-O programs have the essential core competencies to be successful as an I-O practitioner (Huelsman & Shanock, 2020).

In addition, some programs with an international focus may target specific competencies identified by the European Network of Organizational Psychologists (cf. Chapter 3 in this volume by Glazer, Moon, Ayman, and Berger). Furthermore, and as noted by Kottke, Shultz, and Aamodt (2020), I-O master's programs often emphasize the importance of developing professional skills through the completion of internships, practica, and applied course projects. Having a variety of applied organizational experience under the tutelage of faculty supervision ensures some knowledge of organizational politics and builds confidence for the initial job search after graduation.

Waiting on the Platform

After graduate school, I-O master's practitioners will transition through many phases and stages during their career, each presenting opportunities to become socialized and acclimated to a new set of expectations, norms, and organizational realities. Noting the stress and anxiety that may be associated with the major life transition from being a student to becoming a professional, an important task at this pre-application stage for I-O master's students is developing a realistic set of expectations for what will happen next and some concept of the path they would like to pursue as their first of likely many career steps. This challenge involves planning the travel route at least part of the way down the line, to get a sense of the time and distance that will be covered in the foreseeable future. This career forecasting becomes real for most I-O master's students when it is time to seriously engage in the search for employment. Somewhat counterintuitively, a common stumbling block in the initial job search for graduating I-O master's students is the incredible variety of employment options that are available to individuals with an I-O master's degree, training, and related experiences.

One of the most direct pathways to employment is through internship or practicum experiences in which I-O students prove themselves and their competencies and capabilities, securing a job offer by essentially providing a solid work sample and personal proof of concept verifying that the I-O master's student has the skills to function effectively in the workplace. Data from the Survey of I-O Master's Graduates (Shoenfelt, 2019a) indicate that 30.4% of respondents obtained their first professional job with the organization in which they completed their internship. For those who do not get to ride this internship express train to employment and perhaps have not experienced a career job search before, the search process can be daunting and perhaps a hurdle that seems larger than getting into graduate school in the first place. In Chapter 4 in this volume, Walker, Bartels, and Shahani-Denning offered excellent advice on navigating the job application process from application to accepting an offer. One way or another, most graduates of I-O master's programs find and secure I-O related employment within three to six months of graduation (Walker et al., 2020).

Tickets, Please—The Train Has Left the Station

Having secured a berth (i.e., a job) after obtaining an I-O master's degree, a graduate may think it is finally time to settle in for the ride. Nothing could be farther from the truth—a career is about the journey, not the destination. At each stop along this journey, there are opportunities to be on-boarded or socialized into the next period of travel (i.e., new jobs, positions, or organizations, in this context). On-boarding, more formally referred to as organizational socialization, is the process through which workers who are unfamiliar with an organization and its culture, policies, expectations, etc. make the transition from being an external candidate to becoming an contributing incumbent organizational member (e.g., Allen, Eby, Chao, & Bauer, 2017; Bauer & Erdogan, 2011). In most organizations, the initial phase of this process involves completion of administrative paperwork and sharing basic information regarding expectations, policies, and compensation/benefits. If new employees are lucky, this process also will include some mechanism for introducing new hires to their coworkers and supervisors.

Research and theory on socialization suggest that a truly comprehensive on-boarding experience should provide new hires with information about the history, language, politics, people, goals and values, and performance proficiency expectations within the organization (Chao, O'Leary-Kelly, Wolf, Klein, & Gardner, 1994). To accomplish these objectives, on-boarding needs to be seen and experienced as an ongoing process that is more than an orientation event and/or formal training; rather, as a process that also includes continuing support in the new organizational role and encompasses the broader principles of socialization as an open-ended process.

Interestingly, there is no single or even best practice for all of these on-boarding elements. There are reasons to expect that typical organizational socialization methods may fall short for the I-O master's graduate; some of these reasons are grounded in the literature on organizational newcomers as active information seekers (e.g., Bauer, Bodner, Erdogan, Truxillo, & Tucker, 2007; Miller & Jablin, 1991; Morrison, 1993a, 1993b). These researchers have identified a number of ways in which new hires essentially may steer or conduct their own on-boarding. An I-O master's graduate as a new hire is likely to be a stronger active information seeker than a new hire from other, less science-, theory-, and research-driven domains. For organizations, it is important to recognize and support the high need for access to information found in most master's I-O candidates and professionals. We are trained to pursue, acquire, and integrate information from multiple sources. Be aware that someone outside our field may not appreciate our need to develop and proactively exercise the active information-seeking skills that are intrinsic to an I-O psychology way of seeing and interacting with the world. Data from both the I-O Master's Graduate Survey (Shoenfelt, 2019a) and the I-O Masters Employer Survey (Shoenfelt, 2019b), reported in detail later in this chapter, unfortunately indicate insufficient organizational on-boarding. Although most I-O master's graduates reported some form of organizational socialization on job entry, they likewise reported limited access to on-boarding information specifically targeting those with training in I-O psychology; there is room for improvement.

Ideally, socialization is a dynamic process that involves an exchange of effort by the organization and new hires. The goal of socialization is to make newly hired employees feel good about the organization, learn how their job fits within the grand scheme of things, reduce the likelihood of turnover, and acculturate new employees to the norms and values of the company. Organizations typically employ three tactics for socialization (Cable & Parsons, 2001; Van Maanen & Schein, 1979), which are more or less important in successful socialization. *Context* tactics include the delivery of information and targeted activities, *content* tactics target how and when newcomers take their early steps, and *social* tactics address interactions with other organizational members. Lee, Hom, Eberly, and Li (2018) suggested that organizations that strategically use all three tactics for a period of time are more successful in retaining new hires, noting that social tactics have the greatest long-term influence.

Actual socialization practices vary widely across organizations (e.g., Klein & Polin, 2012). Although there is little evidence to support how to best organize the multitude of on-boarding practices, it may be helpful to consider the Inform—Welcome—Guide (IWG) framework to help welcome a newcomer (Klein & Heuser, 2008). Efforts directed at providing information, materials, and potential experiences help to *inform* new hires. This information may be provided through a variety of practices, including several unique or clever on-boarding practices, such as using a life-size board game; scavenger hunts; high-tech videos that focus on culture, community, and/or commitment; and nerd-worthy survival kits that convey the necessities of life within a particular organization (e.g., Bortz, 2017/2018). Such activities are idiosyncratic to a particular company but clearly attempt to convey an investment in people and creativity.

The second type of on-boarding activities, *welcome*, include organizational efforts to introduce new hires and help them feel appreciated and valued by existing organizational members. This category or form of on-boarding is focused more on the development of social capital and facilitating the emotional transition of new hires into the existing organization than on the transfer of technical and/or professional knowledge. To further meet the need for specific knowledge and expertise, the *guide* category of on-boarding practices assists new hires by connecting them directly with "buddies" and mentors to facilitate technical skill development specific to the job and the organization. However, in practice, few on-boarding efforts are designed to differentially address the needs of senior, mid-, and entry-level employees. In fact, responses to the Employer Survey (Shoenfelt, 2019b) suggest that most organizations provide nothing more than a standard orientation.

Within the IWG framework, the important question of which types of on-boarding practices are most effective, for which types of new hires, and for which learning objectives largely remains unanswered. Klein, Polin, and Sutton (2015) explored various types of on-boarding practices, including level of formality versus informality and general effectiveness, and found limited evidence that organizations and employees report the same degree of effectiveness for these boutique practices. The good news is that on-boarding practices are generally viewed as worthwhile, especially when delivered early in a new hire's experience with an organization (Holton, 2001; Klein & Heuser, 2008).

The Klein et al. (2015) findings and the evidence of limited creativity and personalization of on-boarding experienced by most master's I-O professionals lead to important conclusions. We suggest that master's I-O graduates, on their own and with the help of their master's program faculty and alumni, learn and practice strategies for being more proactive when it comes to professional on-boarding. You can begin doing this by thinking about your most recent or imminent job transition and asking yourself how many of the following occurred or are occurring (Caldwell & Peters, 2018):

1. Was a relationship established immediately after hiring, probably through an online presence?
2. Was a mentor appointed to you before your first day onsite?
3. Did any organization members reach out to you soon after hire?
4. Were informational orientation materials provided to you ahead of time?
5. Was your physical workspace and equipment set up for you before you arrived?
6. Were you assisted with the logistics of moving?
7. Did you immediately meet with your supervisor on arrival?
8. Was your transition to the new organization appreciated?
9. Was upper management involved in your training and orientation?
10. Were resources for coaching identified as part of your orientation?

Although not all 10 of these elements may be present in your experience, if you answered "yes" to a good number of these elements, you likely had a welcoming on-boarding process and experienced a degree of prioritization and personalization that is important for transitioning workers of any background. I-O master's graduates can glean additional valuable information by leveraging their master's degree and engaging in their own informal interviewing of incumbents (i.e., organizational subject matter experts) to learn about the incumbents' experience in the organization they are joining.

What happens if one finds that pre-hire expectations are not aligned with the reality of the new position or organization? Explicit and implicit expectations about the nature of the relationship between the new hire and the organization form the psychological contract (Rousseau, 2011). As I-O master's professionals travel, it is prudent to carefully consider what can reasonably be expected from the new position and employer. Delobbe, Cooper-Thomas, and De Hoe (2016) suggested it is likely expectations and this type of psychological contract will develop during socialization. Effective on-boarding practices reflect four foundational concepts: information about your new organization's rules and regulations (*compliance*); a clear expectation of your new job role and expectations for it (*clarification*); a description of the formal and informal organizational norms and values (*culture*); and informational and interpersonal relationships (*connection;* Caldwell & Peters, 2018). Although one should expect to process a large amount of information at the outset of a new job, expect that clarification, culture, and connection will take some additional back-end work. Most organizations do not meaningfully engage new hires at the outset and make assumptions they will pick up these higher-level on-boarding elements on their own. Later socialization experiences are dependent on earlier ones. We are often engaged in tasks and processes in our early development; we not only build on these, we also establish more organizational relationships as we connect with more people over time.

That it may take some work to continue socialization past an initial new employee orientation or training does not assume that the honeymoon period with the new organization is over (Lee, Hom, Eberly, & Li, 2018). Rely on I-O graduate training regarding job attitudes such as satisfaction and organizational commitment that are relational and dynamic. Within the first three months of starting a new work role, new hires likely will experience an unintentional decrease in support from supervisors and coworkers (Kammeyer-Mueller, Wanberg, Rubenstein, & Song, 2013), which, in turn, may negatively affect the inclination to be proactive at work. There are ways to combat this tendency.

When formal socialization programs targeting new hires end, it is important for the new hire to find ways to socialize and engage with other organizational members. Ongoing social interactions facilitate workplace friendships, which can enhance satisfaction, commitment, and productivity (Gallup, 2017), and reduce the possibility of experiencing the dreaded new hire "hangover" (i.e., a dip in job satisfaction occurring a few months post-hire; Wang, Hom, & Allen, 2017). Thankfully, as with other hangovers, its effect should reverse over time as tenure with the organization increases (Son & Ok, 2019). Building and maintaining friendships and other forms of social connections at work can help protect your satisfaction with both your job and the organization.

In addition to promoting more positive personal attitudes about work and the organization, long-term socializing with your coworkers can make it easier for you to ask questions and gather the information needed when questions arise down the line, long after you are no longer considered a new hire. Maintain the mindset of a lifelong learner. Consider on-boarding to be a form of expedited socialization, but recognize that socialization itself is a continual process that extends through your tenure in one organization and spans other organizations as you progress through your career (Klein et al., 2015).

On-boarding Needs and Outcomes for Master's I-O Professionals

Our understanding of on-boarding and socialization improves with each new study published in the area. That said, there are some special needs and challenges for on-boarding programs when their target population is I-O master's professionals. Data from a recent survey conducted for this book, the I-O Master's Graduate Survey (Graduate Survey; Shoenfelt, 2019a), shine some light on the current reality regarding on-boarding, off-boarding, and new employee orientation–type (NEO) socialization experiences for I-O master's graduates. It might be noted that respondents to the Graduate Survey reported graduation years ranging from 1975 to 2018. The median graduation year was 2012; thus, most respondents are relatively recent master's graduates. Some 677 I-O master's graduates responded to the survey item *For what percentage of these positions did you have an opportunity to participate in some form of on-boarding or new employee orientation soon after hire?* The mean response was 64.87% (*SD* = 40.03), but the median was 100%. Thus, most master's graduates reported participating in some form of entry-level socialization experience soon after hire.

At first glance, this rate of socialization is promising. Additional data from respondents to the Graduate Survey (Shoenfelt, 2019a) support the utility and perceived value of these on-boarding/NEO opportunities in the eyes of new hires. Specifically, when asked to indicate the extent to which they found these on-boarding or NEO opportunities to be valuable, 50.6% of respondents indicated the experience was either extremely valuable (19.5%) or very valuable (31.1%), 27.3% indicated the experience was of moderate value, 18.6% reported it to be somewhat valuable, and only 3.5% reported the experience to have no value at all.

Among Graduate Survey respondents who participated in NEO experiences, only 7.9% reported that the experience was specifically tailored to their level of education or contained any content specifically related to their I-O master's training (Shoenfelt, 2019a). This low occurrence of I-O–specific orientation suggests there is room for improvement in on-boarding of I-O master's practitioners with more personalized and tailored upfront education. The few respondents who did experience NEO related to I-O psychology mostly indicated that their organization only or predominantly hired I-O–trained professionals; hence, the on-boarding/NEO was inherently tailored to their I-O training and ability level.

Additional insights about tailored on-boarding may be gleaned from the I-O Master's Employer Survey administered to employers of I-O master's graduates (Shoenfelt, 2019b). Two survey items in particular pertain to on-boarding/NEO experiences. First, 93% of responding employers indicated that when they hire applicants with a master's degree in I-O psychology or a related field, they provide on-boarding or at least some form of NEO for these individuals. This is consistent with the median reported experience of I-O master's graduates (100%), and supports the conclusion that these programs are available.

To probe these experiences a bit further, employers were asked whether these on-boarding/socialization/NEO programs differ in any meaningful way from what is provided to entry-level hires to their organization, and if so, how. Employer responses confirmed the general perception reported by I-O master's graduates, as 75.2% of employers reported they do not tailor their on-boarding/NEO programs in any meaningful way to fit the abilities and needs of I-O master's professionals. The 24.8% of employers who reported customized orientation included the following explanations:

- All new associates attend a general orientation provided by the Learning department. In addition, for our I-O consultants, we have additional on-boarding and training that we conduct within our team to get them up to speed on our projects, tools, etc.
- I-O positions are usually more technical, so on-boarding and training for those individuals is usually more technical. Other entry-level positions would not go into as much detail in training.
- The on-boarding for I-O entry master's graduates is tailored to the data analytic work we perform in our consulting firm along with specific milestones for completion. It is more nuanced and detailed than what would be done for an admin role.

These survey responses suggest there is some recognition by employers that the on-boarding needs of I-O master's graduates are not equivalent to the needs of entry-level workers with other levels or forms of education. However, that so few organizations have NEO experiences tailored to I-O master's graduates suggests most organizations have not invested in a differentiated socialization process for new I-O hires.

Personal Ride Experiences May Differ: Long Distance Versus Subway Transit

Your career will develop as a sequence of related, yet different work experiences. We both have trained many professionals who differ widely in their career aspirations. Some want to explore and travel; they go into external consulting. Some want the security of familiar faces every day; they may enter a particular company or industry. Some expect to sample a little of both internal versus external consulting before they "really" choose. Switching career tracks altogether when new opportunities arise is not uncommon. All, however, shape their careers through their personal journey. As professionals, we instill our self-concepts into careers as a means of self-expression. Career development is a continuous, life-long process that is often disjointed; it features multiple stops and may even require that you switch trains altogether. Expect to take some side trips along the way to your final destination, and do not become concerned if your track deviates a bit from what you originally planned or if the travel is a bit slower than you had anticipated.

Many of our graduates enter their careers at what is known as the *establishment* career stage (Super, 1957). Within Erikson's (1950) stages of development framework, this is roughly a time during which most master's graduates are working through the *identity* versus *role confusion* stage and beginning to struggle with the challenge of *intimacy* versus *isolation*. Despite this intrinsic motivation to achieve some stability and affiliation, it is important to understand that this process can take a while. I-O master's graduates should expect to experience several positions before reaching career stability over a 15- to 20-year period. In fact, the Bureau of Labor Statistics (2015) indicated that later baby boomers (i.e., those born between 1957 and 1964) held an average of nearly 12 different jobs between the ages of 18 and 48. Given recent trends in job transitions and the low unemployment rates experienced for most of the present generation, it is quite likely that recent graduates, especially those with advanced training as in I-O psychology, will experience job changes over the course of their careers. Position changes in the earlier *growth* and *exploratory* stages of the career help to develop interests and skills, and narrowed our choices to I-O; few of us expect to stay in one position for a lifetime. Even after we are established in our careers, there is still an ongoing adjustment process to improve our working situation and position in the *maintenance* stage. And, even though retirement age has recently increased, we engage in preretirement considerations as we enter the *decline* stage of career development.

Stages of career development necessarily parallel those of life stages (cf. Erikson, Maslow, and others); we make work- and non–work-related decisions based on our needs, values, and opportunities. It is important to keep in mind, however, that completion of tasks and goals at each stage is not necessarily a function of age or generation; task completion and goal accomplishment depend more on intelligence and strategic motivation. We must realize our non-work responsibilities and roles are formed by a series of choices, and that all roles we hold affect each other. The combination of roles we choose is essentially the manifestation of and foundation for our identities. We need to understand and appreciate that achieving personal and career fulfillment requires us to pursue, assume, and maintain multiple roles.

Expect a bit more inter-role conflict during the establishment phase of your career as you learn to balance professional career roles (Demerouti, Peeters, & Heijden, 2012). Especially valuable are roles that are personally rewarding, challenging, and meaningful. Given evidence that recent cohorts of students may be even more focused on growth and development than previous generations (Kowske, Rasch, & Wiley, 2010), this message has perhaps never been as important. Thankfully, you can expect life to settle into a rhythm as you find a personal form and level of work and non-work role commitments that are in balance for you, and evolve with you as your career and life progress.

Although career transitions are a reality for working professionals in our field, it is curious and concerning that these experiences do not uniformly come with a comprehensive exit and transition experience. Sturt (2019) stated obvious recommendations for maintaining an ethical work culture in which off-boarding is the norm: Both the organization and the departing employee need to really listen, show appreciation, and stay in touch. In the Graduate Survey (Shoenfelt, 2019a), I-O master's program alumni were asked several questions pertaining to their experiences leaving a work role or organization and any off-boarding that may or may not have occurred. Survey respondents were asked how many I-O positions they have held since completing their I-O master's degree. Among 849 respondents with graduation dates from 1975 to 2018 (*Mdn* = 2012), the mean number of I-O positions held since graduation was 2.64 (*SD* = 1.9; range of 0 to 14). As might be expected, the number of positions held was significantly correlated with the year of graduation ($r = .51, p < .01$) such that those who have been in the workforce longer have held more positions. Among the 367 respondents to this item who graduated in the last five years (i.e., since 2014), the mean number of I-O positions held is 1.75 (*SD* = 1.02), with a range of 0 to 5, and a median of 2 positions.

Some 695 graduates responded to the survey item inquiring if, had they transitioned out of a work role, they had experienced an exit interview (Shoenfelt, 2019a). Among these respondents, 72.5% reported transitioning out of at least one work role, 32.9% indicated they did not experience an exit interview, 40.4% indicated they had transitioned and experienced an exit interview, 26.6% indicated they had never transitioned out of a work role. The strongest forces reported for driving job change were opportunity for growth and development (26%) and salary (20%). Other primary sources of motivation reported for making transitions were organizational culture (15%), work climate (12%), geographic location (12%), work conditions (8%), and other (8%). Other reported reasons for transitioning included issues with supervisors, bosses, or administration; a desire for increased flexibility in one's work; or being laid off by the organization.

Survey respondents were then asked to reflect on off-boarding experiences during their transitions. Responses make it apparent that, although on-boarding may be prevalent, off-boarding is less common. Among 510 respondents who indicated they had transitioned out of a work role, 55.1% indicated they experienced some sort of exit interview; 21.21% indicated they experienced other forms of off-boarding activities or processes. The latter group of respondents provided 100 distinct examples of off-boarding activities or experiences, which we categorized into the following six themes: knowledge transfer activity (34%), exit interview or survey (30%), paperwork or administrative documentation (23%), transition education (10%), recognition for service (2%), and assistance transitioning to self-employment (1%).

Thus, the Graduate Survey responses (Shoenfelt, 2019a) indicate that work-related transitions are common for I-O master's professionals, but these transitions frequently happen without any form of comprehensive off-boarding or role transition experiences. This lack of off-boarding is an important finding given the challenges and strains associated with role transitions in general, and especially between work positions and across work environments (e.g., Ashford, 1988; Metcalfe et al., 2003; Rafferty & Griffin, 2006).

End of the Line?

Careers develop over time, with a need for most I-O master's professionals to "change trains" several times over the course of their postgraduate work lives. Even for individuals who may find their way into the reserved car on a career express train soon after earning their master's degree, there are likely points along the journey where adjustments are needed or new opportunities emerge.

Lessons and Extensions

We see the preceding discussion about socialization and data regarding lack of transition training and off-boarding practices experienced by I-O master's program graduates as a platform for meaningful action. There is an opportunity for I-O master's graduates, I-O graduate programs, and employers of master's I-O professionals to productively collaborate and identify or develop best practices for on-boarding and off-boarding talent. We are continually surprised by how rarely organizations attend to the perspectives and input of departing employees. The relatively low rates of off-boarding observed in our sample of I-O psychology professionals (Shoenfelt, 2019a) belie what is likely an even larger general trend toward ignoring what former employees have to offer about their experience within organizations. We find this troubling when we consider how much insight departing I-O professionals likely could offer their organizations.

Although there is value in exit interviews, our survey data (Shoenfelt, 2019a) are a reminder of the potentially greater value of pre-exit "stay interviews" (e.g., Kaye & Jordan-Evans, 2011; Levoy, 2011; Maddalena, 2015) and other methods of engaging workers in ongoing dialogue regarding what is good and bad about working in an organization. Extending some of the core tenets of the unfolding model of turnover and recent thinking about employee embeddedness (e.g., Lee, Burch, & Mitchell, 2014; Lee, Hom, Eberly, & Li, 2018), organizations are well advised to minimize events that might trigger employees to compare their current work arrangement with potential alternatives. By failing to attend to workers' perceptions of employment alternatives or the events that trigger the development of turnover intentions, organizations are missing valuable opportunities to build organizational resilience and ultimately a stronger culture of retention. This threat can be managed to a large degree by making information readily available for new hires and by encouraging longer-term incumbents to continue to actively seek information, as ongoing social engagement is a way of staying connected to what is happening in the organization.

A relevant issue to raise here is the need for I-O master's graduates to establish realistic expectations about new employment roles and contexts as early as possible in their engagement with an organization. Good socialization and on-boarding programs play an important role in helping to corroborate or abolish newcomers' expectations about their position and the organization. Such programs facilitate evaluation of organizational fit between person and organization, a complex construct that impacts satisfaction, commitment, and turnover intentions (e.g., Kristof-Brown & Guay, 2011). Organizations need to improve the degree and extent to which they share information upfront to help candidates establish realistic expectations. Graduate programs training I-O professionals should teach students what to look for and how to find information that is critical for supporting a smooth transition in their career development.

An additional lesson presented in this chapter is that the developing and changing nature of careers in our field means that I-O master's graduates will experience a sequence of on-boarding and off-boarding. As they work through these cycles, they should keep in mind that off-boarding can inform on-boarding if in these transitions information is shared with the organization. If, as an I-O professional, you are responsible for managing employee socialization in your organization, take steps to facilitate multidirectional information sharing.

The concept of career as a journey should remind us of the importance of not burning bridges and of remembering to send home postcards from the field. Stay in touch with your I-O graduate program roots. In our daily interactions with I-O master's students, we hear frequently of the value associated with opportunities to learn from experienced mentors and to be socialized into the practice of I-O psychology by our program alumni, even when they work in other organizations. The best on-boarding is often delivered through successful mentor connections. You can contribute to the socialization process that affects your profession and you can bring real value to the education of future I-O psychology professionals by sharing your experiences along your career journey.

We hope you found this chapter to be informative, maybe a little thought-provoking, and at least a little bit fun. More than anything, we hope that you can appreciate the value of approaching and experiencing your career as an I-O professional as you might appreciate a scenic train ride. As with any good journey, remember how important it is to share your stories and experiences. As alumni, make time to share your "career travel stories" with others and to reflect on your journey. Remember, it is the journey that matters.

References

Allen, T. D., Eby, L. T., Chao, G. T., & Bauer, T. N. (2017). Taking stock of two relational aspects of organizational life: Tracing the history and shaping the future of socialization and mentoring research. *Journal of Applied Psychology, 102*, 324–337. doi:10.1037/apl0000086

Ashford, S. J. (1988). Individual strategies for coping with stress during organizational transitions. *Journal of Applied Behavioral Science, 24*, 19–36. doi:10.1177/0021886388241005

Bauer, T., Bodner, T., Erdogan, B., Truxillo, D., & Tucker, J. (2007). Newcomer adjustment during organizational socialization: A meta-analytic review of antecedents, outcomes, and methods. *Journal of Applied Psychology, 92,* 707–721. doi:10.1037/0021-9010.92.3.707

Bauer, T. N., & Erdogan, B. (2011). Organizational socialization: The effective on-boarding of new employees. In S. Zedeck (Ed.), *APA handbook of industrial and organizational psychology. Vol. 3: Maintaining, expanding, and contracting the organization* (pp. 51–64). Washington, DC: American Psychological Association. doi:10.1037/12171-002

Bortz, D. (December 2017/January 2018). All on-board. *HR Magazine, 62*(10), 45–49.

Bureau of Labor Statistics. (2015). Number of jobs, labor market experience, and earnings growth: Results from a national longitudinal survey. https://www.bls.gov/news.release/pdf/nlsoy.pdf

Cable, D., & Parsons, C. (2001). Socialization tactics and person-organization fit. *Personnel Psychology, 54,* 1–23. doi:10.1111/j.1744-6570.2001.tb00083.x

Caldwell, C., & Peters, R. (2018). New employee on-boarding—psychological contracts and ethical perspectives. *Journal of Management Development, 37,* 27–39. doi:10.1108/JMD-10-2016-0202

Chao, G. T., O'Leary-Kelly, A. M., Wolf, S., Klein, H. J., & Gardner, P. D. (1994). Organizational socialization: Its content and consequences. *Journal of Applied Psychology, 79,* 730–743. doi:10.1037/0021-9010.79.5.730

Delobbe, N., Cooper-Thomas, H. D., & De Hoe, R. (2016). A new look at the psychological contract during organizational socialization: The role of newcomers' obligations at entry. *Journal of Organizational Behavior, 37,* 845–867. doi:10.1002/job.2078

Demerouti, E., Peeters, M. C., & van der Heijden, B. I. (2012). Work–family interface from a life and career stage perspective: The role of demands and resources. *International Journal of Psychology, 47,* 241–258. doi:10.1080/00207594.2012.699055

Erikson, E. H. (1950). *Childhood and society.* New York: Norton.

Gallup. (2017). *State of the American Workplace.* https://www.gallup.com/workplace/238085/state-american-workplace-report-2017.aspx

Holton, E. F. (2001). New employee development tactics: Perceived availability, helpfulness, and relationship with job attitudes. *Journal of Business and Psychology, 16,* 73–85. doi:10.1023/A:100783980

Huelsman, T. J., & Shanock, L. R. (2020). The I-O master's degree curriculum: Content and modes of delivery for teaching competencies identified in SIOP's *Guidelines for Education and Training in I-O Psychology.* In E. L. Shoenfelt (Ed.), *Mastering industrial-organizational psychology: Training issues for master's level I-O psychologists* (pp. 38–56). New York: Oxford University Press.

Kammeyer-Mueller, J., Wanberg, C., Rubenstein, A., & Song, Z. (2013). Support, undermining, and newcomer socialization: Fitting in during the first 90 days. *Academy of Management Journal, 56,* 1104–1124. doi:10.5465/amj.2010.0791

Kaye, B., & Jordan-Evans, S. (2011). Stay interviews: The leader's role in engaging and retaining talent. *Leader to Leader,* Winter(59), 8–13. doi:10.1002/ltl.448

Klein, H. J., & Heuser, A. E. (2008). The learning of socialization content: A framework for researching orientating practices. In J. Martocchio (Ed.), *Research in personnel and human resources management, Vol. 27* (pp. 279–336). Bingley, UK: Emerald Group Publishing Limited. doi:10.1016/S0742-7301(08)27007-6

Klein, H. J., & Polin, B. (2012). Are organizations on board with best practices on-boarding? In C. R. Wanberg (Ed.), *Oxford handbook of organizational socialization* (pp. 267–287). New York: Oxford University Press. doi:10.1093/oxfordhb/9780199763672.013.0014

Klein, H. J., Polin, B., & Sutton, K.L. (2015). Specific on-boarding practices for the socialization of new employees. *International Journal of Selection and Assessment, 23,* 263–283. doi:10.1111/ijsa.12113

Kottke, J. L., Shultz, K. S., & Aamodt, M. G. (2020). Importance of applied experiences: Course projects, practica, simulations, and internships. In E. L. Shoenfelt (Ed.), *Mastering industrial-organizational psychology: Training issues for master's level I-O psychologists* (pp. 57–77). New York: Oxford University Press.

Kowske, B., Rasch, R., & Wiley, J. (2010). Millennials' (lack of) attitude problem: An empirical examination of generational effects on work attitudes. *Journal of Business and Psychology, 25,* 265–279. doi:10.1007/s10869-010-9171-8

Kristof-Brown, A., & Guay, R. P. (2011). Person–environment fit. In S. Zedeck (Ed.), *APA handbook of industrial and organizational psychology. Vol. 3: Maintaining, expanding, and contracting the organization* (pp. 3–50). Washington, DC: American Psychological Association. doi:10.1037/12171-001

Lee, T. W., Burch, T. C., & Mitchell, T. R. (2014). The story of why we stay: A review of job embeddedness. *Annual Review of Organizational Psychology and Organizational Behavior, 1*(1), 199–216. doi:10.1146/annurev-orgpsych-031413-091244

Lee, T. W., Hom, P., Eberly, M., & Li, J. C. (2018). Managing employee retention and turnover with 21st-century ideas. *Organizational Dynamics, 47,* 88–98. doi:10.1016/j.orgdyn.2017.08.004

Levoy, B. (2011). The stay interview. *Optometric Management, 46*(10), 95.

Maddalena, L. L. (2015). "Stay" interviews. *Credit Union Management,* November, 50–52.

Metcalfe, C., Smith, G. D., Sterne, J. A. C., Heslop, P., Macleod, J., & Hart, C. (2003). Frequent job change and associated health. *Social Science & Medicine, 56,* 1–15. doi:10.1016/S0277-9536(02)00005-9

Miller, V., & Jablin, F. (1991). Information seeking during organizational entry: Influences, tactics, and a model of the process. *Academy of Management Review, 16,* 92–120. doi:10.5465/amr.1991.4278997

Morrison, E. W. (1993a). Longitudinal study of the effects of information seeking on newcomer socialization. *Journal of Applied Psychology, 78,* 173–183. doi:10.1037/0021-9010.78.2.173

Morrison, E. W. (1993b). Newcomer information seeking: Exploring types, modes, sources, and outcomes. *Academy of Management Journal, 36,* 557–589. doi:10.5465/256592

Rafferty, A. E., & Griffin, M. A. (2006). Perceptions of organizational change: A stress and coping perspective. *Journal of Applied Psychology, 91,* 1154–1162. doi:10.1037/0021-9010.91.5.1154

Rousseau, D. M. (2011). The individual–organization relationship: The psychological contract. In S. Zedeck (Ed.), *APA handbook of industrial and organizational psychology. Vol. 3: Maintaining, expanding, and contracting the organization* (pp. 191–220). Washington, DC: American Psychological Association.

Shoenfelt, E. L. (2019a). I-O master's graduate survey. Survey conducted for E. L. Shoenfelt (Ed.) (2021). *Mastering the job market: Career issues for master's level industrial-organizational psychologists.* New York: Oxford University Press.

Shoenfelt, E. L. (2019b). I-O master's employer survey. Survey conducted for E. L. Shoenfelt (Ed.) (2021). *Mastering the job market: Career issues for master's level industrial-organizational psychologists.* New York: Oxford University Press.

Society for Industrial and Organizational Psychology, Inc. (2016). *Guidelines for education and training in industrial/organizational psychology.* Bowling Green, OH: Author.

Son, J., & Ok, C. (2019). Hangover follows extroverts: Extraversion as a moderator in the curvilinear relationship between newcomers' organizational tenure and job satisfaction. *Journal of Vocational Behavior, 110*, 72–88. doi:10.1016/j.jvb.2018.11.002

Sturt, D. (2019, May 21). Your company needs a process for off-boarding employees gracefully. *Harvard Business Review.* https://hbr.org/2019/05/your-company-needs-a-process-for-off-boarding-employees-gracefully

Super, D. E. (1957). *The psychology of careers: An introduction to vocational development.* Oxford, UK: Harper & Bros.

Van Maanen, J., & Schein, E. H. (1979). Toward a theory of organizational socialization. In B. M. Staw (Ed.), *Research in organizational behavior* (pp. 209–264). Greenwich, CT: JAI.

Wang, D., Hom, P. W., & Allen, D.G. (2017). Coping with newcomer "hangover": How socialization tactics affect declining job satisfaction during early employment. *Journal of Vocational Behavior, 100*, 196–210. doi:10.1016/j.jvb.2017.03.007

6

Professional Development for Industrial-Organizational Psychology Master's Graduates

Joseph J. Mazzola, Donna Chrobot-Mason, and Cody B. Cox

Professional development is a vital aspect of the career of industrial-organizational (I-O) psychology master's graduates, particularly early in their careers as they move into the working world and establish themselves. Education does not end when one walks across the graduation stage; those who fail to seek and capitalize on professional development opportunities risk being left behind, stagnating in their career projection. This chapter focuses on some of the best ways professionals in the field can continue to add to their toolbox after they have finished their formal I-O education.

Continuing Education

The I-O Master's Graduate Survey and Employer Survey (Shoenfelt, 2019a, 2019b) found that a large number of I-O master's graduates sought to obtain additional qualifications after earning their degree in I-O psychology. To wit, approximately two-thirds (65.6%) sampled in the Employer Survey reported that their employees engage in ongoing training and development opportunities each year. Within that sample, one of the most common opportunities mentioned were certificate programs; namely, more than one-third (36.6%) of employers reported their master's I-O employees pursued a graduate certificate subsequent to earning their degree.

Joseph J. Mazzola, Donna Chrobot-Mason, and Cody B. Cox, *Professional Development for Industrial-Organizational Psychology Master's Graduates* In: *Mastering the Job Market*. Edited by: Elizabeth L. Shoenfelt, Oxford University Press (2021). © Society of Industrial and Organizational Psychology. DOI: 10.1093/oso/9780190071172.003.0006

Considering Certificates

The relatively high number of I-O master's graduates pursuing certificates is not surprising given the increasing number of certificate programs available nationally. Indeed, the number of post-baccalaureate and post-master's degrees/certificates awarded by colleges and universities has doubled from 2002 (when fewer than 30,000 were awarded) to 2017 (more than 60,000; NCES, n.d.). In its first 18 months alone, over 8,000 people completed Google's IT certificate for entry-level positions (McKenzie, 2019). Two of the most popular fields overall for certificates are health care and business operations (Cronen, McQuiggan, Isenberg, & Grady, 2017). Thus, as certificates become more common and available, especially those relevant to I-O psychologists, it is not surprising that I-O master's graduates would avail themselves to these opportunities to grow their skills and to build their résumé.

The certificates reported by the Graduate Survey sample (Shoenfelt, 2019a) covered a variety of areas. Many respondents reported participating in traditional areas of certification such as the Senior Professional in Human Resources (SPHR) and the Professional in Human Resources (PHR; ~17%). Another 11% reported participating in the Society of Human Resource Management (SHRM; shrm.org) certifications, and 6% reported participating in other human resources (HR) areas. Interestingly, approximately 5% of I-O master's respondents reported becoming a Certified Compensation Professional specifically or completing certification in payroll and compensation more generally. These results suggest that credentialing in traditional HR areas is popular among I-O master's graduates, who completed certificates in a wide variety of topics, presumably ones that are most relevant to their roles and career goals.

In addition to HR, Six Sigma training was relatively popular; more than 15% of graduate respondents reported receiving some Six Sigma training. Among the subsample reporting Six Sigma training, there was a fairly even split between Six Sigma and Lean Six Sigma training. Despite some discussion about Six Sigma becoming less common (e.g., Davenport, 2008), this certification remains relatively popular with I-O master's-level psychologists. Six Sigma is not an area traditionally covered in I-O curriculum; I-O programs may want to consider including this area in their curriculum as some I-O graduates seek out these experiences after graduation. Similarly, although not specifically a certificate, Toastmasters could be a useful club for those who have issues with presentations and interpersonal exchanges (www.toastmasters.org).

Assessments likewise was a popular area of professional development for I-O master's survey respondents. Overall, about 8.6% of participants reported receiving some training in assessments. A few respondents reported certifications in MBTI, DISC, or Birkman specifically, but Hogan Assessment Certification was the most popular, with 5.6% reporting that they obtained some form of Hogan Certification. Training was comparatively less popular; only 3.5% reported completing some form of Association of Training Development (ATD) certificate. Project management was also mentioned by the participants; 5% participated in Project Management Professional certification. Another 4% reported participating in change management certifications, and 2% reported completing some form of strategic workforce planning certification. In sum, these findings suggest that additional training and certifications in selection and assessment are popular among I-O master's-level practitioners.

It was somewhat surprising that relatively few participants reported pursuing certificates related to statistics or research. Only approximately 4.6% of our I-O master's graduate sample obtained certificates related to statistics and 3.2% obtained a certificate related to analytics. A few participants reported pursuing certificates in R or SAS; however, other programs, such as SPSS and Mplus, were not mentioned. In general, participants were far more likely to pursue certificates in areas related to HR generally or assessment specifically than in statistics or research methods. Although there may be other ways to interpret these findings, several explanations seem most relevant. First, it may be that I-O master's programs are providing significant and sufficient training in statistical methodology for their students, so students do not need to seek additional training beyond their graduate coursework. Second, it may be that advanced statistical methods are not as relevant for master's-level I-O psychologists in the workforce as other training may be. Finally, some I-O master's-level practitioners may find some of these advanced topics intimidating and experience "statistical anxiety" (Siew, McCartney, & Vitevitch, 2019). As such, these individuals may choose not to pursue these particular certifications, preferring to maintain jobs and projects where these skills are not necessary. Indeed, I-O psychologists may at times get pushback from managers on the importance and utility of advanced statistical methodology, since organizations continue to struggle to implement data-driven culture (Bean & Davenport, 2019). Whatever the reason, I-O master's graduates reported obtaining certifications in statistical methods less frequently than other certifications.

Finally, there were some other areas of certification and credentialing that were less easily categorized. Among these miscellaneous areas, coaching was the most popular: 5% of the I-O master's graduates reported receiving credentialing in coaching. A few participants reported receiving safety training (including certificates from the Occupational Safety and Health Administration [OSHA]), training to use LinkedIn, and diversity recruitment. These trainings may reflect niche areas within I-O psychology where specialization may be particularly important. These trainings also may reflect an increasing incorporation of technology into I-O psychology; in particular, the use of LinkedIn and other social media resources in hiring and recruiting may become an increasingly important area in which I-O psychologists pursue additional training.

Overall, I-O master's graduates pursued a wide variety of certificates. Although the results of the Graduate Survey (Shoenfelt, 2019a) contained a considerable amount of variability, there were some general trends. First, I-O psychologists are more likely to pursue certificates in traditional HR areas (particularly the PHR and SPHR) than in areas related to research or statistics. Whether this is due to career demands or availability of these programs is not clear, but these results suggest that I-O practitioners may need additional training in more traditional HR areas than I-O master's programs are currently providing. Although many programs do include a course in HR management (HRM) or talent management, providing additional courses or instruction may be beneficial for students. Further, there was a surprising amount of interest in change management relative to other areas, perhaps reflecting the increased popularity of change management and organization development alongside more traditional I-O psychology content.

Other Means of Continuing Education

I-O graduates can increase both their competencies and marketability by improving and updating their methodological or statistical skills through courses or continuing education. As mentioned previously, few participants in the Graduate Survey (Shoenfelt, 2019a) reported obtaining statistical/analytical certificates. However, it is possible this lack of certification is partially due to obtaining such knowledge and skills from smaller courses or presentations. For example, many current I-O practitioners likely graduated before R was a dominant statistical package and, as such, may seek to learn this program through an online tutorial or seminar. The Consortium for Advancement of Research Methods and Analysis (CARMA; carmattu. com) is a great resource for continuous learning opportunities in analytics. Although access to the CARMA site typically requires a fee, paid by either the individual or an organization, individuals have access to a wide variety of live and archived videos on a number of statistical/methodological concepts. CARMA also offers free access to a limited number of archived webcasts. Respected members of the field frequently serve as CARMA instructors and, in 2019, offered seminars on topics such as panel data, dirty data, and big data analytics. LinkedIn also provides courses directly on its website; participants can then directly link their new skills on their profile and résumé (linkedin. com/learning).

The Society of Industrial and Organizational Psychology (SIOP; siop. org) offers a number of opportunities to enhance current knowledge in the field. The Leading Edge Consortium (siop.org/Leading-Edge-Consortium) is an annual event with prominent I-O psychologists presenting on topics of key interest. The annual SIOP conference provides a variety of opportunities to develop skills and earn continuing education credits, including preconference workshops. The Leading Edge Consortium and the annual SIOP conference are just a few of the many ways in which I-O master's graduates can add knowledge and skills to their toolkit through SIOP.

Additional Degrees

Although continuing education credits or certificates may be sufficient for some I-O master's practitioners, others may seek further professional development by completing a second or third degree. A master's in business administration or HR management might complement the I-O master's degree and enhance marketability. Programs that combine a psychology and business degree are becoming more common (college.lovetoknow.com/ Psychology_MBA_Combination_Degree), Specifically, some schools now offer dual-degree programs where students leave with I-O master's and MBA degrees at graduation (examples include Roosevelt University and Appalachian State University). Of course, professionals can return to school to add a degree without using dual-degree programs. Earning an additional degree while employed full time as a working professional has become easier given the plethora of online and evening programs, and many organizations will reimburse some tuition and education-related expenses. Other I-O master's graduates may specialize in HR management or data analytics as a means of further enhancing their marketability for specific jobs. However, only 7% of respondents in the Graduate Survey reported that they had also obtained an MBA, MPS, or HRM degree. Thus, although such degree combinations are being offered, the Graduate Survey results suggest that most I-O master's graduates find their I-O master's degree to be sufficient for their career goals.

Finally, some I-O master's-level psychologists decide later in their career to pursue a PhD. This decision is based on you, your current job/field, and your aspirations; a doctorate can open doors not available to I-O master's graduates (e.g., academic or consulting positions) and/or can replace a certain number of years of experience required for a job. Pursuing a doctorate can occur at any point in an individual's career journey; one author of this chapter can attest to teaching a new PhD student who was in their 60s! Individuals considering such a move should seek out relevant information (e.g., Landers, 2011) and weigh the usefulness of the degree versus the economic, intellectual, and time investments required.

Wise Choices for Continuing Education

Unfortunately, there is no "right" answer to the question of which certifications an I-O master's graduate needs. The earlier discussion about common certificates obtained by I-O master's graduates, both in terms of how/where the certificates are offered and the topics they cover, is a useful starting point. We recommend reflecting on your career aspirations and determining what certificates others in your specific area currently possess as a guideline for potential certifications as you seek additional knowledge/skills and potential advancement. The heterogeneous nature of I-O psychology makes the identification of "universal certifications" impossible but likewise suggests a wide variety of potentially helpful certificates.

We strongly recommend determining the credibility of the university, program, and/or organization offering a certificate as, unfortunately, some certificate programs are designed mostly for profit purposes and may provide little value to students (Marcus, 2017). Seeking information about how applicable and useful the certificate will be is vital as well, as additional degrees often are not necessary for career advancement. Before undertaking a major career transition, investigate if and when an additional degree might be useful, and whether the degree is worth the significant investment of resources required. A career mentor's perspective, discussed later in this chapter, can be an important asset in determining what continuing education opportunities are worthwhile and getting the most out of the time and resources you invest in professional development opportunities.

Ultimately, it is up to you to ensure that you invest wisely in your professional development. Continuing education workshops, conferences, webinars, and other presentations are usually lower in terms of resource commitment than are advanced degrees or certificates. Each of these methods of professional development can be useful; wise choices can help ensure that you target the right skills to aid career advancement and to add useful skills to your toolbox.

Mentoring

The Importance of Mentoring for I-O Psychologists

Finding and maintaining relationships with mentors is an important component of an I-O psychologist's ongoing professional development. Mentoring is a developmental relationship between a more experienced person (aka mentor) and a less experienced protégé. Such a relationship is distinguished by an explicit focus on career learning, development, and growth (Ragins, 2016). In positive or high-quality mentoring relationships, both partners have high responsiveness, trust, and emotional attachment to each other and the relationship. High-quality mentoring relationships offer a number of benefits to both the mentor and protégé. Benefits reported in the literature include higher salaries, increased promotion rates, greater career satisfaction, higher organizational commitment, and less intention to leave the organization as well as lower levels of turnover (Murrell, Blake-Beard, Porter, & Perkins-Williamson, 2008).

Because as I-O psychologists we espouse to be scientist-practitioners, we may benefit significantly by having multiple mentors to meet a variety of personal and professional needs. For example, you may wish to consider finding a mentor who is an academic/scholar, a practitioner within your organization, and another working outside your organization, someone of the same race and gender, as well as someone of a different race and gender. Indeed, mentoring scholars advocate for having multiple mentors because each may provide a unique set of benefits (Murrell et al., 2008). For example, mentors similar to one's self in terms of race, gender, family status, expertise, etc. may be able to provide psychosocial support and offer advice on navigating some of the unique challenges they have faced in the workplace. Likewise, mentors who are quite different from one's self can offer very different insights and perspectives that may be equally beneficial. Mentors with different professional expertise and social contacts may provide their protégés with the unique opportunity to network with a more diverse group of professionals, which results in broader access to new ideas and perspectives as well as strategies for overcoming obstacles (Chrobot-Mason, Cullen, & Altman, 2013; Cullen, Gerbasi, & Chrobot-Mason, 2018; Murrell et al., 2008).

Some mentoring relationships may be characterized as formal in nature; because formal relationships are promoted or organized by the organization, the mentor and protégé may be assigned to one another, and there are specific parameters or goals established by the organization for the relationship (Baugh & Fagenson-Eland, 2007). In contrast, informal mentoring relationships develop spontaneously based on mutual connection and interpersonal comfort. As such, informal mentoring relationships are more likely to last longer and be of greater benefit to both the mentor and the protégé (Baugh & Fagenson-Eland, 2007). That being said, both types of relationships can be beneficial, and it is the quality of the relationship that seems to matter more than the type (Ragins, Ehrhardt, Lyness, Murphy, & Capman, 2017).

Survey data collected from graduates of I-O master's programs reveal that, when entering the workforce, less than half (43%) of the respondents surveyed had a mentor who helped them get started in their career (Shoenfelt, 2019a). Those who did have a mentor, however, typically commented on how important that relationship was to them in their development. One respondent stated, "My mentor helped me learn how to transition into the work world from an academic world, how to navigate politics, how to present and talk to executives." Another said, "She allowed me a lot of autonomy, while also providing guidance and feedback when I needed it." Respondents revealed that their mentors were most often a supervisor or direct boss. In some cases, though, their graduate program advisor became a professional mentor after graduation. The length of time for mentoring relationships varied widely, from a few months to 25 years and counting. Somewhat surprisingly, more I-O graduates report acting as a mentor to others in the field of psychology (55%) than receiving mentorship themselves (43%).

In examining data from the Employer Survey (Shoenfelt, 2019b), we found that informal mentoring was more prevalent than formal mentoring programs. Of the 98 respondents, only 31% reported that formal mentoring programs were common in their organization and 49% indicated that they had acted as a formal mentor to others in the workplace. In contrast, 79% reported that informal mentoring was common in their organization, and an overwhelming 86% reported that they had acted as an informal mentor to others in the workplace. Comments reveal perceived benefits to both. For example, one respondent suggested that "informal mentoring seems to be more effective because it is based on creating and maintaining a relationship vs. following prescribed material." Another stated that "formal mentoring allows us to more closely track progress and outcomes and helps us to design better programs." Overall, the survey data suggest that informal mentoring is more prevalent, and it can be more effective in developing lasting relationships built on trust and can better serve a protégé in terms of providing specific advice and support in advancing one's career. Formal mentoring, however, may be more effective for on-boarding during that crucial time period where the new employee needs guidance and support but has not yet developed relationships to establish an informal mentoring relationship.

Best Practices for Mentoring

Considering the mentoring literature as well as the data collected from our survey research, three pieces of advice emerge for master's-level I-O psychologists.

Find and Be a Mentor

A clear picture emerges from decades of research on mentoring: Mentoring provides significant benefits in terms of personal learning and growth for both mentors and protégés (Ragins, 2016). Although mentoring of any kind requires a commitment of both time and emotions, such investments can be greatly rewarding if the relationship is of high quality. Recent research suggests that mentors may serve a critical role as a buffer to negative workplace interactions and experiences such as both direct and indirect discrimination and bias. Mentors can serve as a buffer and help to mitigate the negative impact of such events because they can offer both empathy and perspective to the protégé (Ragins et al., 2017).

However, less than half of our survey respondents reported that they had a mentor when they entered the workforce. There may be many reasons behind this low statistic. One reason may be that the field of I-O psychology has not emphasized the benefits of mentoring enough or educated students about strategies for finding an informal mentor. Thus, this information may need to be provided and/or more strongly emphasized in our graduate programs. Another reason for this low number may be the result of not having what many would consider to be an effective or appropriate mentor in the organization. Many I-O psychologists may mistakenly believe that they need to find a mentor who is also an I-O psychologist, which leaves them in many cases without a mentor, leading to our next suggestion.

Find Multiple Mentors

As we pointed out earlier, I-O psychologists can benefit greatly by seeking multiple mentoring relationships with people in multiple fields, areas of expertise, and organizations. Many may find that they are the only I-O psychologist in the organization and, thus, may experience some feelings of isolation. One strategy for overcoming such feelings is to purposefully and strategically seek out mentoring relationships with multiple people to serve multiple needs (Cullen-Lester, Woehler, & Willburn, 2016). For example, you may seek a relationship with one mentor who has a strong external network; another mentor may be the person you turn to when you need a confidence boost or someone to vent with; finally, a third mentor may be an expert in a certain competency area and can help you develop a specific skill. It is difficult, if not impossible, to find a single mentor to meet all of our professional development needs; nor is it wise to expect any single person to fulfill so much. One mentor may be familiar with the certificates and tools that are necessary for career advancement, while another might best understand navigating the politics in your organization. Indeed, it is wiser to seek out multiple mentors in order to best leverage their unique strengths and contributions, which leads to our third suggestion.

Find Diverse Mentors

Decades of research tell us that we naturally seek out people like ourselves; this remains equally true when seeking mentors or selecting protégés

(Cullen-Lester et al., 2016). We feel most comfortable around people we deem to be most like us, which results in a natural inclination to seek out mentors who are similar to ourselves in terms of race, gender, educational background, family status, religion, political affiliation, etc. However, the research is also clear that there are tremendous benefits associated with cultivating diverse relationships in the workplace (Chrobot-Mason et al., 2013; Cullen et al., 2018; Murrell et al., 2008). Diverse mentors can help us understand challenges and obstacles from different perspectives, can introduce us to people outside of our own network who may be valuable sources of information and experience, and can also help us grow in our understanding and advocacy for a more inclusive workplace.

In summary, our data suggest that I-O psychologists are generally underusing mentoring as a professional development practice and strategy. As such, we challenge readers to develop a mentoring team composed of many diverse individuals and organizations and to actively reach out to others and volunteer to be a mentor. The benefits of doing so will far outweigh the costs.

Staying Connected

Finally, an I-O master's graduate may wish to continue professional development simply by staying connected to the field in a variety of ways after graduation. One of the primary ways for I-O master's professionals to remain connected to the field is by joining SIOP and participating in SIOP events. Although SIOP membership historically has been composed mostly of doctoral-level I-O psychologists, more recently, as the number of master's-level I-O graduates has increased, SIOP has placed increased emphasis on attracting more master's graduates to the organization, and making membership and conferences more appealing to them. I-O master's graduates can join SIOP as associate members. In 2015, SIOP approved a pathway to full membership for associate members who hold an I-O master's degree and meet several other eligibility requirements.

There are other related professional organizations that many I-O master's practitioners choose to join, such as SHRM and ATD. As previously mentioned, SHRM, ATD, and other organizations offer certificates that may develop additional knowledge and skills and increase marketability for I-O master's graduates. These professional organizations host a variety of events as well, many of which might benefit I-O master's graduates.

Another way graduates can stay involved in the field of I-O psychology is by connecting with local I-O organizations. SIOP membership is an important way to stay in touch with colleagues and continued trends, but local organizations allow for direct networking in one's geographical area, learning about work opportunities, and giving back to students and the community. The SIOP website provides links to more than 60 organizations on its "Local I-O Groups and Related Organizations" page (siop.org/membership/local-I-O-groups). Examples include Chicago I-O Psychologists (CIOP) and North Carolina I-O Psychologists (NCIOP). Local I-O groups host events such as speakers, mixers, and conferences for students, academics, and practitioners to come together for networking and learning. We highly recommend that I-O master's graduates affiliate with local I-O organizations or, if one doesn't currently exist in their area, that they consider starting a local I-O group such as the recently created Louisville I-O Network (LION).

Hosting events for organizations or students is another avenue for I-O master's graduates to stay connected to the field and with local colleges and graduate students. For instance, the Center for Creative Leadership (Cullen et al., 2014) routinely hosts the NCIOP conference. Such programs enable organizations and I-O practitioners to give back, as well as to network with other local I-O professionals and graduate students. Such networking could lead to an organization finding their next great intern or employee, or to I-O practitioners finding their next position.

There are many ways for I-O psychologists to network, and there is no one best method for doing so. Individuals have different styles and comfort levels with networking activities. In addition, individual differences in introversion/extraversion, social anxiety, and shyness make networking more or less pleasant. Research indicates that 60% to 90% of people find their job through networking (psychology.iresearchnet.com/industrial-organizational-psychology/group-dynamics/networking/), which suggests that general networking and staying connected through at least some avenues is vitally important. In-person networking can happen in many of the venues mentioned in this chapter, such as conferences, local organizations, seminars/talks, and even certificate/continuing education classes. Employees can enhance their virtual networking through the websites of the organizations mentioned here. Websites such as LinkedIn have become more and more important for networking in today's workforce (Waddington, 2012).

Conclusion

Professional development, in whatever form it takes, is important for practitioners in any field. Continuous learning is particularly important for I-O psychology practitioners given our focus on the dynamic and constantly growing body of workplace science, as well as the perceived scientist-practitioner divide (Caetano & Santos, 2017). We strongly encourage I-O master's graduates to seek professional development throughout their careers. There are a myriad of opportunities for continuous learning, as highlighted throughout this chapter, that not only add value to one's résumé but also add more tools to one's toolbox and further enrich I-O practitioners as both individuals and professionals.

References

Baugh, S. G., & Fagenson-Eland, E. A. (2007). Formal mentoring programs: A "poor cousin" to informal relationships? In B. R. Ragins & K. E. Kram (Eds.), *Handbook of mentoring at work: Theory, research, and practice* (pp. 249–272). Thousand Oaks, CA: Sage.

Bean, R., & Davenport, T. H. (2019, February). Companies are failing in their efforts to become data-driven. *Harvard Business Review.* https://hbr.org/2019/02/companies-are-failing-in-their-efforts-to-become-data-driven

Caetano, A., & Santos, S. C. (2017). The gap between research and professional practice in work and organizational psychology: Tensions, beliefs, and options. In E. R. Neiva, C. Vaz Torres, & H. Mendonça (Eds.), *Organizational psychology and evidence-based management: What science says about practice* (pp. 1–22). Cham: Springer International Publishing. https://doi-org.proxy108.nclive.org/10.1007/978-3-319-64304-5_1

Chrobot-Mason, D., Cullen, K., & Altman, D. (2013). Leveraging networks through boundary spanning leadership. In J. Nickerson & R. Sanders (Eds.), *Tackling wicked government problems: A practical guide for developing enterprise leaders* (pp. 101–115). Washington, DC: Brookings Institution Press.

Cronen, S., McQuiggan, M., Isenberg, E., & Grady, S. (2017). https://www.insidehighered.com/sites/default/server_files/files/2017103_2016%20ATES%20First%20Look%20Report_for508c_090617.pdf

Cullen, K., Wilburn, P., Chrobot-Mason, D., & Palus, C. (2014). Networks: How collective leadership really works. White paper published by the Center for Creative Leadership. *Cutting-edge Thought Forum Insights.*

Cullen, K. L., Gerbasi, A., & Chrobot-Mason, D. (2018). Thriving in central network positions: The role of political skill. *Journal of Management, 44*(2), 682–706. doi:10.1177/0149206315571154

Cullen-Lester, K. L., Woehler, M. L., & Willburn, P. (2016). Network-based leadership development: A guiding framework and resources for management educators. *Journal of Management Education, 40,* 321–358. https://doi.org/10.1177/1052562915624124

Davenport, T. H. (2008, January 8). Why Six Sigma is on the downslope. *Harvard Business Review*. https://hbr.org/2008/01/why-six-sigma-is-on-the-downsl

iResearchNet. Networking. https://psychology.iresearchnet.com/industrial-organizational-psychology/group-dynamics/networking/

Landers, R. (2011, June). Grad school: Should I pursue a Ph.D. or Master's in I/O Psychology. *NeoAcademic*. http://neoacademic.com/2011/06/14/grad-school-should-i-get-a-ph-d-or-masters-in-io-psychology/

Marcus, J. (2017, October). A college certificate may not be the clear pathway to a job. *NBC News*. https://www.nbcnews.com/news/education/college-certificates-may-not-be-clear-pathway-job-n813511

McKenzie, L. (2019, June 14). Google's growing IT certificate. *Inside Higher Education*. https://www.insidehighered.com/digital-learning/article/2019/06/14/google-it-certificate-program-expands-more-community-colleges

Murrell, A. J., Blake-Beard, S., Porter, D. M., & Perkins-Williamson, A. (2008). Interorganizational formal mentoring: Breaking the concrete ceiling sometimes requires support from the outside. *Human Resource Management, 47*(2), 275–294. doi:10.1002/hrm.20212

National Center for Education Statistics (NCES). (n.d.). Degrees and certificates awarded: How many degrees/certificates are awarded at postsecondary institutions? https://nces.ed.gov/ipeds/TrendGenerator/app/answer/4/24?f=33%3D8%7C6

Ragins, B. R. (2016). From the ordinary to the extraordinary. *Organizational Dynamics, 45*(3), 228–244. doi:10.1016/j.orgdyn.2016.07.008

Ragins, B. R., Ehrhardt, K., Lyness, K. S., Murphy, D. D., & Capman, J. F. (2017). Anchoring relationships at work: High-quality mentors and other supportive work relationships as buffers to ambient racial discrimination. *Personnel Psychology, 70*(1), 211–256. doi:10.1111/peps.12144

Shoenfelt, E. L. (2019a). I-O master's graduate survey. Survey conducted for E. L. Shoenfelt (Ed.) (2021). *Mastering the job market: Career issues for master's level industrial-organizational psychologist*. New York: Oxford University Press.

Shoenfelt, E. L. (2019b). I-O master's employer survey. Survey conducted for E. L. Shoenfelt (Ed.) (2021). *Mastering the job market: Career issues for master's level industrial-organizational psychologist*. New York: Oxford University Press.

Siew, C. S. Q., McCartney, M. J., & Vitevitch, M. S. (2019). Using network science to understand statistics anxiety among college students. *Scholarship of Teaching and Learning in Psychology, 5*(1), 75–89. http://dx.doi.org/10.1037/stl0000133

Waddington, J. (2012). *Share this: The social media handbook for PR professionals*. Hoboken, NJ: John Wiley & Sons.

7

Professional Identity of Industrial-Organizational Psychology Master's Graduates

Mark S. Nagy, Shahnaz Aziz, and Daniel A. Schroeder

When Doug Reynolds became president of the Society for Industrial and Organizational Psychology (SIOP) in 2012, his primary goal was to improve the branding, or the professional identity, of industrial-organizational (I-O) psychology.[1] He recognized that there was little to distinguish the practice of I-O psychology from other professional fields. Unfortunately, this lack of identity persists. Recently, the Association of State and Provincial Psychology Boards (ASPPB), an organization that provides guidance to jurisdictions in the United States and Canada regarding the licensure of psychologists, updated its "Model Act" that may be used by jurisdictions to set their licensure policy. The revision of the Model Act included the following language:

> This act is for the regulation of the practice of psychology only and does not prevent human resource professionals, business consultants, and other persons from providing advice and counseling in their organizations or affiliated groups or to their companies and employees of their companies or from engaging in activities performed in the course of their employment. (p. 21)

Thus, this Model Act suggests that there may be little difference between I-O psychologists and human resource professionals, business consultants, or other professionals. Although this Model Act was meant to allow professionals trained in I-O psychology to continue to practice (as long as they do not refer to themselves as "psychologists"), one could argue that the Act detracts from establishing the professional identity of I-O psychologists.

Mark S. Nagy, Shahnaz Aziz, and Daniel A. Schroeder, *Professional Identity of Industrial-Organizational Psychology Master's Graduates* In: *Mastering the Job Market.* Edited by: Elizabeth L. Shoenfelt, Oxford University Press (2021).
© Society of Industrial and Organizational Psychology. DOI: 10.1093/oso/9780190071172.003.0007

Furthermore, such language does little to distinguish between doctoral graduates and master's graduates in I-O psychology.

Hence, the purpose of this chapter is to discuss the professional identity of master's-level I-O psychology graduates. First, licensure trends within I-O psychology will be discussed, followed by the distinction between licensing and certification/credentialing, and how certification may be an avenue to removing barriers to licensure while also helping the field of I-O psychology establish a brand or identity. Finally, we present a discussion of professional membership, including reasons for joining a professional organization as well as the results of the I-O Master's Graduate Survey (Shoenfelt, 2019a), which was conducted specifically for this volume. We conclude with thoughts on what our professional identity may be and how it potentially can be crystallized in the future.

Licensing Trends in I-O Psychology

Licensing is a significant issue in the professional practice of psychology, including I-O psychology. Individuals considering a career as an I-O psychologist need to understand the emerging trends regarding this issue and continue to stay current over the course of their careers. Doing so will help them to effectively navigate the choppy terrain associated with licensing.

Context/Background

First, we provide some context on the licensing issue. Licensure has grown through the decades. Currently, approximately 29% of the workforce in the United States is licensed (Licensing Joint Task Force of the ASPPB, 2017). At the same time, with the rise of visible and impactful special interest groups such as the American Legislative Exchange Council, an anti-regulatory perspective has emerged in the United States. Many legislatures within the United States are pursuing "anti–red tape" agendas. As a result, many psychology boards are now required to promulgate only those rules for which they have explicit statutory authority. This means that the details of these statutes and rules are being carefully revisited and revised, and will continue to be as time unfolds.

Historically, although there has been variation across the United States for licensure as a psychologist, typical requirements have included (1) a doctoral degree in psychology or a substantially equivalent degree, (2) supervised experience by a licensed psychologist(s), and (3) a passing score on the Examination for the Professional Practice of Psychology. Many jurisdictions also require a passing score on a jurisdiction-specific ethics or jurisprudence examination. Most licensing jurisdictions govern both the practice of psychology and the use of the title "psychologist."

Interestingly, in recent years, increased attention has been given to the credentialing associated with the professional practice of psychology at the master's level (Buckman, Nordal, & DeMers, 2018; Grus & Skillings, 2018; Hughes & Diaz-Granados, 2018). Increasingly, individuals with terminal master's degrees offer psychological services. Accordingly, the regulation and licensure of master's-level practitioners in psychology has been an emerging area of research, investigation, and discourse. We envision that this trend will continue and that, in the future, licensure implications for master's-level practitioners will be identified and corresponding recommendations for pathways to licensure will be promulgated.

Model Acts

Within the context of licensing trends, it is important to note that two major bodies associated with the professional practice of psychology (i.e., the American Psychological Association [APA] and the ASPPB) have published Model Acts outlining suggestions for "best practices" in licensing (APA, 2010; ASPPB, 2010). Both Model Acts recognize the increasing diversity of professional psychology and these two main groupings: (1) health services psychologists (HSPs) and (2) applied consulting psychologists (ACPs) or general applied psychologists (GAPs). I-O psychologists fall into the latter category. Recognizing that the education, training, and supervised experience vary between HSPs and ACPs/GAPs, both Model Acts suggest that psychology boards take these differences into account regarding revisions to statutes and rules.

It is important to note that the professional practice of psychology (i.e., the areas of psychology for which licensure is recommended) encompasses both HSP and ACP/GAP areas of application as distinct practice areas. The

American Board of Professional Psychology, a board-certifying body for licensed doctoral-level psychologists, identifies the following specific practice areas: (1) behavioral and cognitive psychology, (2) clinical child and adolescent psychology, (3) clinical health psychology, (4) clinical psychology, (5) clinical neuropsychology, (6) counseling psychology, (7) couple and family psychology, (8) forensic psychology, (9) geropsychology, (10) group psychology, (11) organizational and business consulting psychology, (12) police and public safety psychology, (13) psychoanalytic psychology, (14) rehabilitation psychology, and (15) school psychology (American Board of Professional Psychology, 2019).

While using slightly different nomenclature, APA identifies the following specific practice areas: (1) clinical neuropsychology, (2) clinical health psychology, (3) psychoanalysis in psychology, (4) school psychology, (5) clinical psychology, (6) clinical child psychology, (7) counseling psychology, (8) industrial-organizational psychology, (9) behavioral and cognitive psychology, (10) forensic psychology, (11) geropsychology, (12) police and public safety psychology, (13) sleep psychology, (14) rehabilitation psychology, and (15) group psychology and group psychotherapy (APA, 2019). Additionally, the APA recognizes three proficiencies: (1) addiction psychology, (2) sport psychology, and (3) biofeedback and applied psychophysiology.

We envision these practice areas (and areas that emerge in the future) as the focus of the licensing statutes and rules that are promulgated throughout the United States. The manner in which the statutes and rules address ACPs/GAPs and I-O psychologists in particular will be something for I-O psychology educators, students, and practitioners to monitor closely. How the licensure matter evolves over time will inevitably impact the field of I-O psychology in terms of modification or recalibration of educational and training programs and the pathways to be pursued in the professional practice of I-O psychology.

It should be noted that within SIOP, licensing is a controversial issue that evokes rigorous debate among SIOP members (cf., Campbell, 2017; Licensure of Consulting and I-O Psychologists [LCIOP] Joint Task Force, 2017; Locke, 2017; Tippins, 2006). SIOP recently revised the following policy on licensure (SIOP, 2019): "SIOP recognizes that many states require that the practice of I-O psychology be licensed. SIOP members should be allowed to be licensed in those states that require such licensure, and SIOP should provide guidance to state licensing boards on how to evaluate the education and training of an I-O psychologist."

The Current Situation

The U.S. Department of Labor (2019a, 2019b) currently identifies psychology as an occupation that is growing and has a bright outlook. Given that the professional practice of psychology requires graduate-level educational preparation, enrollments in graduate programs in psychology have increased over the past few years (Jones, 2018). The composition of the student population in those graduate programs has become increasingly diverse along the way (Educational Testing Service, 2016).

With regard to specific licensure practices, a 2017 study by the LCIOP Joint Task Force of ASPPB documented that five states restrict licensure to HSPs: Georgia, Hawaii, Illinois, New Mexico, and Utah. The same study identified five states that exempt non-HSPs from licensure: Hawaii, Illinois, North Carolina, South Dakota, and Wyoming. Additionally, the study documented that 14 states require graduation from a program accredited by the APA or the Canadian Psychological Association: Washington, DC, Florida, Georgia, Iowa, Kansas, Maryland, Massachusetts, Mississippi, Nebraska, North Dakota, Oklahoma, Pennsylvania, Tennessee, and Utah. The study also reported that six states do not have a generic license: Colorado, Washington, DC, Hawaii, Illinois, New Mexico, and Utah.

Licensure for the professional practice of psychology continues to be a focus of attention by legislators, academicians, and practitioners. There are some encouraging signs that variations in licensure practices across the jurisdictions are lessening. Recent work by the ASPPB, discussed in the next section, has been foundational along these lines.

PSYPACT and E.Passport

In April 2019, ASPPB's Psychology Interjurisdictional Compact (PSYPACT) became operational (ASPPB, 2016, 2019a). This was a significant event because PSYPACT is an interjurisdictional compact specifically designed to facilitate the professional practice of telepsychology and the temporary face-to-face practice of psychology across state lines.

In its finished form, ASPPB's PSYPACT will provide psychologists with a process and certificates for offering temporary practice across state lines. ASPPB, via an E.Passport, will also provide psychologists with a process and certificates for offering telepsychology services (ASPPB, 2019b). The

E.Passport is a certification process that is part of ASPPB's Mobility Program. It requires an applicant to submit evidence supporting education, licensure, and successful completion of the Examination for the Professional Practice of Psychology. Once granted, three hours of professional development in the area of the use of technology in psychology are required for renewal of the certificate.

Via its PSYPACT, ASPPB will promote further cooperation and standardization of requirements among psychology boards. Subsequently, over time, this standardization has the potential to improve access to psychological services while protecting consumers.

In light of the foregoing discussion, we envision that the licensure issue for I-O psychologists, including master's-level practitioners, will continue to evolve. Fueled by PSYPACT, we foresee increasing clarity, consistency, and cooperation among the psychology boards within the jurisdictions of the United States for licensing and credentialing of both doctoral-level and master's-level practitioners, including I-O psychologists. We are optimistic that the historical terrain of confusing and varied licensing practices for psychologists within the United States will be replaced by an elegant, efficient, and effective process that can be readily modified and enhanced over time to be responsive to emerging needs and challenges. Importantly, however, the issue of licensure is quite different from the issues of certification and credentialing.

Certification and Credentialing

Those in I-O psychology may confuse the terms and practices of licensure, credentialing, and certification. In reality, however, as we will discuss, at least two of these credentials are quite different and have extremely important legal and practice implications.

Licensure

Although some have proclaimed that licensure restricts free trade, restricts membership in a profession, and actually protects a profession from competition rather than protecting the public (e.g., Kleiner & Krueger, 2013; Locke, 2017), the act of licensure is determined not by a profession but by state and provincial legislators. That is, licensure is determined by the enactment of state and provincial laws. Hence, violating a licensure regulation essentially is breaking a law. For this reason, violating a licensure law is significantly more severe than violating a certification or credential.

The core issue of licensure in any field, including I-O psychology, is to protect the public from potential harm. Thus, if the practice of some profession has the potential to inflict harm on the general public, that profession may be a candidate for licensure. In some settings, public protection is easy to determine. For instance, medical and legal professionals have the potential to inflict harm on the public, so those professions require licensure in order to practice. Two areas more closely related to I-O psychology that require licensure to practice are clinical and counseling psychology. It is argued here that professionals who engage in sensitive and potentially impactful discussions, such as those involving the disclosure of personal information and vulnerabilities, have the potential to inflict harm if these professionals are not competent.

Yet, the question of whether I-O psychologists can inflict harm on the general public may not be as clear, even among those who have been educated in the field of I-O psychology. For instance, among respondents to the I-O Master's Graduate Survey conducted for this volume (Shoenfelt, 2019a), 39.8% disagreed or strongly disagreed with the statement that, "Individuals or organizations (could) be harmed if someone without advanced I-O psychology training tried to do (their) work." However, 39.0% agreed or strongly agreed with this statement and about 21% neither agreed nor disagreed with the statement. Thus, about half of the respondents who had an opinion agreed that the work performed by those trained in I-O psychology has the potential to harm the public. Interestingly, the percentage of respondents who agreed that I-O work can harm the public was significantly higher in a 2011 SIOP membership survey that asked respondents to indicate their level of agreement with the statement, "Individuals and/or their employer organizations could be harmed in some way (e.g., experience financial or emotional distress) if someone without advanced training in I-O psychology tried to do my work"; 64% responded with *strongly agree* or *agree*. More recently, Shen (2016) found that 68% of CSIOP members reported that harm could be inflicted on the public if others without appropriate I-O psychology training attempted to do their work. Additionally, Axton, Porr, Dumani, and Ferro (2016) reported that respondents to the 2015 Practitioner Needs Survey (distributed by SIOP) indicated that the potential for causing harm was either *very likely* (60%) or *somewhat likely* (29%) if someone without advanced training tried to do their work. Hence, a majority of SIOP members believe that the activities typically performed by I-O psychologists have the potential to harm the public.

These survey findings from SIOP members suggest that, by the public harm standard, I-O psychologists should be licensed. And, despite a near 50/50 split on the potential for public harm on the I-O Master's Graduate Survey, 58.3% of these respondents indicated they would apply for licensure if the requirements were more appropriate for master's graduates (Shoenfelt, 2019a).

Despite the perception that I-O psychologists have the potential to harm the public and the apparent desire by a majority of master's graduates to pursue licensure if possible, SIOP's official policy on licensure simply states that SIOP should help those who want to become licensed (SIOP, n.d.a). Yet, this policy is misleading as it implies that it is up to individuals to determine if they should be licensed (Nagy & Schroeder, 2019). As noted earlier, the decision of whether one needs to be licensed is not made by the individual; it is determined by legislators in each licensing jurisdiction. Unfortunately, there are quite a few barriers to licensure for those trained in I-O psychology, including education, supervision, and continuing education requirements (Blanton & Nagy, 2012). Consequently, we recommend that the SIOP leadership endorse legislation that reduces these barriers for those trained in I-O psychology to be eligible for licensure.

Certification/Credentialing

One approach to potentially remediate at least some barriers to licensure for I-O professionals is to explore the process of certification and/or credentialing. Blanton and Nagy (2012) authored a white paper on how barriers to licensure for GAPs (which include I-O psychology–trained professionals) could be overcome and, with the help of the ASPPB, distributed that paper to all licensing boards. Unfortunately, little change to licensure eligibility for GAPs occurred. Hence, another approach to helping licensing boards evaluate the eligibility of GAPs for licensure could be the establishment of a certification in I-O psychology. Because certification and credentialing share many similar characteristics, these two terms will be used interchangeably in the remainder of this chapter. Unlike licensure, which is a legal issue and is controlled by those outside of the profession (i.e., legislators, and state and provincial psychology licensing boards), certification and/or credentialing is a practice that is often under the control of those in a given profession. For instance, the Society for Human Resource Management (SHRM) awards two different certifications, a Professional in Human Resources (PHR) and a Senior Professional in Human Resources (SPHR). Those seeking SHRM certification must meet educational and experiential requirements and take an exam that was developed with the help of SHRM members; those who pass the exam become certified. Thus, not only does certification involve an exam that is created by those in the profession (SHRM members), but the decision to grant certification also is determined by the professional organization.

In our opinion, that the profession controls the certification process would be the greatest advantage to instituting a certification program for I-O psychologists. The standards required for certification could be determined by SIOP members (or leadership), the requisite certification exam could be developed by SIOP members, and the awarding of certifications could be controlled by SIOP. Unlike licensure standards, which are determined by boards of psychology that often comprise only those trained in other areas of psychology (or often not trained in psychology at all), the educational and competency standards for certification (or credentialing) in I-O psychology would be determined by SIOP.

Currently, approximately 14 jurisdictions require licensure candidates to have graduated from an APA-accredited graduate program. As it stands now, APA only accredits clinical, counseling, and school psychology graduate programs; it does not accredit I-O psychology programs, which effectively precludes anyone trained in I-O from pursuing a psychology license. Thus, a second advantage of I-O certification is that such a designation potentially could be used to assist state and provincial boards when making decisions regarding licensure eligibility, particularly for individuals who did not graduate from an APA-accredited program. Certification in I-O psychology could be used by licensing boards such that, when evaluating licensure eligibility of those trained in I-O psychology, I-O certification could stand in lieu of graduating from an APA-accredited program. As such, an I-O certification would reduce an educational barrier to licensure for I-O psychologists.

Despite these advantages to certification (or credentialing), there are disadvantages. One major drawback of certification is that it does not solve other potential barriers to licensure, such as supervision and continuing education requirements. Accordingly, requirements for I-O psychology certification may need to include supervision or experiential standards in addition to a certification exam. Such a certification would be strengthened if continuing education was required to maintain one's certification. Certification programs accredited by the National Commission for Certifying Agencies typically require that certification applicants meet appropriate educational and experiential requirements, pass a certification exam, and complete ongoing continuing education to maintain certification. Certification programs accredited by the National Commission for Certifying Agencies typically require adherence to a professional code of ethics. Developing a certification program is an arduous process that entails significant time, effort, and financial expenditure by the professional organization sponsoring the program.

Another disadvantage of certification is that licensure is a legal framework controlling the title and practice of psychology and, as such, is enforceable by law; certification is not. Furthermore, the terms "psychology" and "psychologist" could not be used in the title of an I-O certification. Thus, professionals certified in I-O psychology but not licensed could still engage in potentially illegal behavior by using the title "psychologist." Hence, it is conceivable that certification could lead to increased confusion among those who practice I-O psychology.

Future Identity of I-O Psychology Master's Graduates

The current lack of certification or licensure in I-O psychology is ironic because those trained in I-O psychology have knowledge of the scientific method and advanced statistics; this knowledge is not found in the training of similar professionals such as human resources professionals or MBAs. Such I-O psychology training makes master's-level graduates better suited to solve organizational problems with evidence-based approaches than those trained in other areas that lack these skills. Despite these advantages, it appears the field of I-O psychology has failed to capitalize on the advanced training and education received by those in the profession by failing to require some demonstration of competencies that could distinguish I-O psychology from other professions.

Yet, this distinction would serve the field of I-O psychology well, as the general public seems to have little understanding of what those trained with a master's degree in I-O psychology do, and/or are capable of doing (e.g.,

Gasser, Whitsett, Mosley, Sullivan, Rogers, & Tan, 1998). That is, it appears the field of I-O psychology lacks a "brand." According to businessdictionary. com, a *brand* is a "unique design, sign, symbol, words, or a combination of these, employed in creating an image that identifies a product and differentiates it from its competitors. Over time, this image becomes associated with a level of credibility, quality, and satisfaction in the consumer's mind." In other words, a brand is an identity that is communicated to others. If relatively few people know what a master's graduate in I-O psychology does, then as a field we have a lot of work ahead to communicate to others what we do.

In our opinion, one way to establish an I-O brand is to ensure that those earning a master's degree in I-O psychology receive training that is largely consistent across graduate programs. Unfortunately, there is little consistency in the courses that are required across I-O psychology master's programs (Tett, Walser, Brown, Simonet, & Tonidandel, 2013). In fact, the SIOP *Guidelines for Education and Training in Industrial and Organizational Psychology* (SIOP, 2016) recognize considerable heterogeneity among graduate programs (Huelsman & Shanock, 2020). The Guidelines take a competency-based approach to graduate training and leave the methods for development of core competencies to individual graduate programs. The Guidelines further state that they are not standards, that the recommendations contained therein are not mandatory or enforceable, and that they do not serve the purpose of preparing individuals for licensure or certification. Yet, without consistent training across master's graduate programs, it is difficult for the field of I-O psychology to establish a brand because the messaging of what a person earning an I-O master's degree is capable of doing would be inconsistent. Hence, by developing a certification in I-O psychology, SIOP could establish the educational requirements and standards for certification; consequently, I-O psychology master's programs likely would align their educational training with the certification educational requirements and exam content. It must be noted, however, that such educational training standards should allow enough room for individual I-O psychology programs to specialize within a subspecialty such as compensation or occupational safety and health.

The future identity of those trained with a master's degree in I-O psychology must begin by distinguishing themselves from other professionals in related fields. This distinction should emphasize the specialized training of I-O psychology master's graduates, particularly in the areas of the scientific method and advanced statistics. Further, this distinction can be enhanced by creating a certification in I-O psychology under the auspices of SIOP. Such a certification would likely result in I-O psychology master's programs offering, if not requiring, courses that meet the requirements for certification. Moreover, such a certification may be used to assist state and provincial licensing boards in determining eligibility for candidates who wish to become licensed in the field of I-O psychology. If SIOP were to institute a certification program, getting employers to recognize and require such certification could prove to be a challenging hurdle. In the I-O Master's Employer Survey (Shoenfelt, 2019b), when employers were asked whether any professional certifications were required or preferred for I-O master's employees, most employers indicated they were neither required nor preferred. Only the SHRM PHR or SPHR certifications were mentioned by multiple employers as preferred certificates (see Chapter 4 in this volume by Walker, Bartels, and Shahani-Denning).

Another avenue for determining the professional identity of I-O master's graduates is to examine their memberships in various professional organizations.

Membership in Professional Organizations

Perhaps one of the most gratifying experiences for I-O master's graduates, whether academicians or applied professionals, is being affiliated with professional organizations and attending their meetings. SIOP touts itself as the premier professional organization for the science and practice of I-O psychology. It is an independent, self-governed organization that retains representation of APA Division 14, and it is affiliated with the Association for Psychological Science. SIOP's mission is "to enhance human well-being and performance in organizational and work settings by promoting the science, practice, and teaching of industrial-organizational psychology" (SIOP, n.d.b).

SIOP provides many services to its 10,000+ members across the globe. Student memberships are available; those with an I-O master's degree may join SIOP as an associate member. In 2015, SIOP created a pathway to full membership for master's-level I-Os to make SIOP more inclusive of master's graduates. Associate members who meet the requirements of SIOP engagement are given access to professional member status with the full benefits of membership, including the right to vote in SIOP elections and to serve as a committee chair or on the executive board. Through a wide range of activities, SIOP supports its members in their efforts to model and reinforce the effective integration of science and practice through teaching, research, and application of the principles, theories, and methods of I-O psychology (SIOP, n.d.b).

Respondents to the I-O Master's Graduate Survey (Shoenfelt, 2019a) were asked to indicate SIOP membership; 77.9% said they belonged to SIOP as a graduate student. Those who indicated they currently belong to SIOP fell into the following categories: 6.0% as a student affiliate, 13.7% as an associate member, 12.0% as a member, 0.1% as a SIOP fellow, and 0.1% as a retired member. That close to half of I-O master's student members forgo their SIOP membership after graduation is a concern. Other survey items explored possible explanations for this attrition from SIOP.

Survey respondents who do not belong to SIOP were asked to check reasons why they are not SIOP members. They provided the following reasons for deciding not to join SIOP: Employer does not pay for membership (19.8%); no value of joining it (18.8%); membership cost is too expensive (18.5%); using social media (e.g., LinkedIn, Facebook, Twitter) to network (16.9%); other professional organizations are better aligned with professional duties (15.3%); using Google to do quick searches to get answers to questions (12.1%); conference registration fees and related travel costs are too expensive (10.1%); other professional organizations provide better value (7.2%); and people do not join professional organizations anymore (2.8%). That nearly half of the respondents (48.4%) identified some form of cost as a reason for not belonging to SIOP suggests SIOP may need to explore reduced fees for recent I-O master's graduates to encourage their membership. In addition, 41.3% indicated SIOP does not meet their professional needs.

Respondents to the Graduate Survey (Shoenfelt, 2019a) indicated various reasons for being SIOP members. The most frequent response was the SIOP annual conference (17.4%), followed by professional development (13.0%); access to resources (e.g., mentoring, workshops, IOP journal, *Newsbriefs*; 12.9%); networking opportunities (11.7%); listservs (e.g., I-O Job Network, consultant locator, social media, teaching resources; 4.7%); leadership experience (e.g., serve on governing boards, executive committees; 2.4%); SIOP Fall Leading Edge Consortium (1.8%); and, finally, research grants, scholarship, and award funds (0.8%).

The SIOP annual conference is regularly attended by more than 4,000 SIOP members representing 110 countries. The SIOP conference features over 800 peer-reviewed sessions across the three-day meeting that target both academicians and practitioners representing excellence in education, research, and practice of I-O psychology. The sessions are designed to contribute to organizational effectiveness and the well-being of individual employees (SIOP, n.d.b). Among Graduate Survey respondents who are SIOP members, 31% indicated they regularly attend (i.e., at least once every three years) the SIOP annual conference; however, only 2.6% indicated they regularly attend the SIOP Fall Leading Edge Consortium (Shoenfelt, 2019a).

Typically, annual conferences are held in exciting locales. SIOP recently held meetings at attractive venues such as Austin, Chicago, Orlando, and Philadelphia, with upcoming conferences in New Orleans and Seattle. Moreover, at the conference, there are colleagues and friends to catch up with, sights to soak in, and, of course, a plethora of knowledge to be gained. Yet, professional organizations and meetings might be intimidating to the novice I-O graduate student, recent master's graduates, or even junior faculty members. SIOP I-O Ambassadors is a program that matches experienced conference-goers with newcomers to the conference to ease the transition into conference attendance.

Reasons for Joining a Professional Organization

A common question in the context of professional organizations is why one should become a member. Here we discuss in more detail the benefits of membership in professional organizations for I-O master's graduates. An early consideration is the cost of joining a professional organization. Even though SIOP annual membership dues are quite reasonable (i.e., currently $110 annually), expensive membership fees, potential increased annual dues, and expensive conference registration fees (even with early registration discounts) indicate this concern is certainly valid. Among respondents to the Graduate Survey (Shoenfelt, 2019a) who do not belong to SIOP, various costs of membership and conference attendance accounted for 48.4% of the reasons cited for not joining SIOP. Yet, being affiliated with a professional organization provides numerous benefits, as we will discuss.

Resources

Professional organizations offer their members access to a variety of resources. SIOP member benefits include a subscription to *Industrial and
Organizational Psychology: Perspectives on Science and Practice (IOP)*, the official quarterly journal of I-O psychology. IOP contains interactive exchanges
on topics that are essential to the science and practice of I-O psychology. The
format of the journal is focal article–peer commentary in nature, whereby
peer-reviewed focal articles are presented to SIOP members via email notification when each focal article is available on the SIOP website; those who are
interested may submit a commentary to be considered for publication.

The Industrial-Organizational Psychologist (TIP) is a digital, quarterly
news publication that includes articles, news, and reports pertaining to the
association and the profession. Current and past issues of *TIP* are available
for open access on the SIOP website. *Newsbriefs*, a monthly newsletter sent
electronically to SIOP members, contains the latest information about I-O
psychology and work-related behavior, as well as updates on matters relevant
to SIOP (e.g., proposed bylaws amendments for consideration by members,
call for nominations for Foundation awards).

Although likely of more interest to I-O master's faculty than master's
graduates, another resource provided by professional organizations is
mentoring programs in which junior scholars are matched with senior
scholars who provide guidance and support, as well as opportunities to network. SIOP and some other professional organizations have teaching resources, continuing education, and salary information available, as well
as professional development resources such as conference submission
templates. In addition, faculty may find ideas for innovative research and
publication by attending conferences where cutting-edge research facilitates
exposure to emerging trends in practice and research.

Facilitation of Job Searches

Employers frequently post job ads for discipline-specific positions on professional organization websites. The SIOP website contains the I-O Job
Network, where employers may post positions for a small fee and job seekers
may search at no cost postings for a wide variety of positions and internships.
Discipline-specific websites such as the I-O Job Network facilitate finding
appropriate positions for job seekers when compared to searches on extensive databases such as *The Chronicle of Higher Education* or online job
posting sites such as Glassdoor, Indeed, etc. In addition, some employers use

the SIOP Conference Placement Center to meet and conduct preliminary interviews with job candidates at the annual conference.

Networking

Membership in SIOP offers unique opportunities for networking through the annual conference or the Leading Edge Consortium, where leaders in the field of I-O psychology are in attendance and presenting. Informal meetings at these venues may lead to future collaborations and/or provide an "in" to a job opportunity. In addition, professional organizations' social media platforms provide an avenue for networking with others in the discipline; SIOP provides networking opportunities through SIOP social media. Members can further network and serve SIOP through elected offices and volunteer committee positions. To further serve members, SIOP offers a media resources database, a SIOP consultant locator service, and free résumé postings in the I-O Job Network. Many larger metropolitan areas have local I-O groups that provide opportunities to network with other I-O professionals in one's geographical area, discuss current issues, hear presentations, obtain career advice and mentoring, and, potentially, even discover a job lead (SIOP, n.d.c).

Awards, Grants, Fellowships, and Scholarships

Most professional organizations, including SIOP, provide opportunities to earn awards, grants, and scholarships, which may be useful in one's career progression. Awards recognize accomplishments in teaching, research, and/or practice; grants are awarded to fund high-potential research or practice; and scholarships are awarded to graduate students to assist with funding for thesis or dissertation research, or conference travel.

The SIOP Foundation supports applied organizational science via excellence in teaching, research, and practice through grants, awards, and scholarships available exclusively to SIOP members. As of December 2018, the SIOP Foundation reported cumulative award distributions of more than $1 million and endowments of over $4 million (SIOP, 2019). The naming of a SIOP fellow recognizes outstanding contributions to the I-O discipline. Each form of recognition is highly competitive; thus, any of these honors should be valued beyond the fact that it enriches one's résumé or curriculum vitae. SIOP honors more than 70 award recipients with recognition at the annual conference plenary session; these recipients also are highlighted in emails and newsletters throughout the year. At the conference, SIOP award recipients and newly elected fellows are invited to attend a dessert reception with Foundation donors. Award winners are further recognized at the conference reception in conjunction with the networking reception and top posters.

Leadership Experience

Last but not least, membership in a professional organization provides the opportunity to serve in a variety of roles and to acquire leadership experience. Most professional organizations operate through various committees and governing boards run by member volunteers. It serves both the member and the organization to participate in these opportunities. Gaining leadership experience in a professional organization provides wisdom in terms of the inner workings of the organization; assists with becoming acquainted with other leaders, which may in turn lead to additional professional opportunities; and is a résumé builder. Serving on one of the more than 30 standing and ad hoc SIOP committees is a valuable service to the Society and enhances one's knowledge about the issues confronting SIOP and its members. Participation in the SIOP Media Resources Directory provides opportunities to present I-O issues in the media. SIOP Student Affiliates can volunteer to assist at the annual conference at the registration desk, in the exhibit hall, giving directions, etc. (SIOP, n.d.c). Volunteering provides a new perspective on SIOP membership and enhances the membership experience in a number of ways. Yet, among Graduate Survey respondents who belong to SIOP, only 2.5% indicated they currently serve on a SIOP committee; 4.9% have served on a SIOP committee in the past (Shoenfelt, 2019a).

Membership in Other Professional Organizations

Roughly 30% of I-O master's graduate are members of professional organizations other than SIOP (Shoenfelt, 2019a). Specifically, Graduate Survey respondents indicated memberships in SHRM (17.4%), APA (3.7%), Association for Talent Development (3.0%), American Society for Training and Development (1.7%), Academy of Management (1.6%), Association for Psychological Sciences (1.0%), Organizational Development Network (0.6%), Society for Occupational Health Psychology (0.5%), American Association for Public Opinion Research (0.5%), American Compensation Association (0.5%), World at Work (0.5%), International Personnel

Assessment Council (0.4%), Market Research Association (0.4%), Society for Consulting Psychology (0.3%), Society for Professionals in Management (0.1%), and other (e.g., American Society for Quality [0.2%] and Association of Test Publishers [0.2%], to name a few). Thus, I-O master's graduates belong to SIOP at a higher rate (31.9%) than to any other professional organization. SHRM is SIOP's greatest competitor in terms of I-O master's graduate members (17.4%). It is quite likely that some I-O master's graduates belong to multiple professional organizations.

Graduate Survey respondents (Shoenfelt, 2019a) provided the following reasons for their membership in organizations other than SIOP: professional development (22.9%); access to resources (18.9%); networking opportunities (17.6%); employer requested it and/or paid for it (10.8%); annual conference (7.4%); leadership experience (4.6%); research grants, scholarship, and award funds (0.8%); and listservs (2.0%). Finally, 31% of respondents indicated they regularly attend (i.e., at least once every three years) another professional organization's conference. Some 8.7% of respondents indicated they serve on another professional organization's committees. These responses suggest SIOP might explore offering professional development opportunities specifically targeting I-O master's graduates if it is interested in increasing their membership in SIOP.

Conclusion

According to the results of the I-O Master's Graduate Survey (Shoenfelt, 2019a), a majority of I-O master's graduates were members of SIOP as graduate students (77.9%), but far fewer (31%) attend the SIOP annual conference regularly, and just as many (31%) attend other professional conferences. These findings suggest that many of those trained with a master's degree in I-O psychology may begin to lose their professional identity as I-O psychology master's graduates as they become involved in their career. Clearly, maintaining membership in SIOP and attending the annual SIOP conference would be key to establishing a professional identity in I-O psychology.

Perhaps another way to increase the professional identity of those trained in I-O psychology at the master's level would be for SIOP to establish a certification process similar to those found in other professional fields, such as the PHR and SPHR certifications offered by SHRM. Such a certification process could be developed internally (i.e., by SIOP) and, consequently, the requirements for certification could help those trained in I-O psychology maintain their identity as an I-O professional. A certification program may result in more consistent training of master's I-O students, which would further enhance the professional identity of I-O master's graduates. Finally, it is suggested that such certification could remove barriers to licensure for doctoral- and master's-level graduates trained in I-O psychology and could be used to help jurisdictions determine proper eligibility requirements for licensure. As PSYPACT continues to be adopted by states, increased cooperation among psychology boards as well as increased consistency for licensure standards could allow for more I-O professionals to become licensed, further solidifying the professional identity of I-O professionals.

Note

1. The information in this chapter is based on previous work by the first and third authors published as Nagy, M. S., & Schroeder, D. A. (2019). Emerging issues in the licensure of I-O psychologist: Part I. *The Industrial and Organizational Psychologist, 56*(4). Copyright © The Society for Industrial and Organizational Psychology, www.siop.org, reprinted by permission of SIOP.

References

American Board of Professional Psychology. (2019). *Specialty boards.* Chapel Hill, NC: Author. https://www.abpp.org/Applicant-Information/Specialty-Boards.aspx

American Psychological Association. (2010). *Model act for state licensure of psychologists.* Washington, DC: Author.

American Psychological Association. (2019). *Recognized specialties and proficiencies in professional psychology.* Washington, DC: Author. https://www.apa.org/ed/graduate/specialize/recognized

Association of State and Provincial Psychology Boards. (2010). *ASPPB model act for licensure and registration of psychologists.* Peachtree City, GA: Author.

Association of State and Provincial Psychology Boards. (2016). *Psychology interjurisdictional compact (PSYPACT).* Peachtree City, GA: Author. https://cdn.ymaws.com/www.asppb.net/resource/resmgr/psypact_docs/Psychology_Interjurisdiction.pdf

Association of State and Provincial Psychology Boards. (2019a). *PSYPACT becomes operational.* Peachtree City, GA: Author. https://www.asppb.net/news/448039/PSYPACT-becomes-Operational.htm

Association of State and Provincial Psychology Boards. (2019b). *E.Passport quick guide.* Peachtree City, GA: Author. https://cdn.ymaws.com/www.asppb.net/resource/resmgr/psypact_docs/e.passport_quick_guide_v.10.pdf

Axton, T. R., Porr, B., Dumani, S., & Ferro, M. (2016). Licensing and industrial-organizational psychologists: Member needs and news. *The Industrial and Organizational Psychologist, 54*(1). http://www.siop.org/tip/july16/license.aspx

Blanton, J. S., & Nagy, M. (2012). *Licensing issues for consulting and industrial-organizational psychologists.* Unpublished manuscript. Cincinnati, OH: Xavier University.

Buckman, L. R., Nordal, K. C., & DeMers, S. T. (2018). Regulatory and licensing issues derived from the summit on master's training in psychological practice. *Professional Psychology: Research and Practice, 49*(5-6), 321–326.

Campbell, J. P. (2017). Licensing of I-O psychologists: Some potentially lethal features. *Industrial and Organizational Psychology: Perspectives on Science and Practice, 10,* 190–193.

Educational Testing Service. (2016). *Key trends in graduate and professional education: Attracting students in changing times.* Princeton, NJ: Author. https://www.ets.org/s/gre/pdf/ihe-key-trends-graduate-and-professional-education.pdf.

Gasser, M., Whitsett, D., Mosley, N., Sullivan, K., Rogers, T., & Tan, R. (1998). I-O psychology: What's your line? *The Industrial-Organizational Psychologist, 35*(4), 120–126.

Grus, C. L., & Skillings, J. L. (2018). Scope of practice considerations related to master's training and psychological practice. *Professional Psychology: Research and Practice, 49*(5-6), 311–313.

Huelsman, T. J., & Shanock, L. R. (2020). The I-O master's degree curriculum: Content and modes of delivery for teaching competencies identified in SIOP's *Guidelines for Education and Training in I-O Psychology.* In E. L. Shoenfelt (Ed.), *Mastering industrial-organizational psychology: Training issues for master's level I-O psychologists* (pp. 38–56). New York: Oxford University Press.

Hughes, T. L., & Diaz-Granados, J. (2018). Master's summit: Quality assurance and accreditation. *Professional Psychology: Research and Practice, 49*(5-6), 306–310.

Jones, L. (2018). Study reveals notable graduate school enrollment trends. *Diverse Issues in Higher Education.* https://diverseeducation.com/article/128255/

Kleiner, M. M., & Krueger, A. B. (2013). Analyzing the extent and influence of occupational licensing on the labor market. *Journal of Labor Economics, 31,* S137–S202.

Licensure of Consulting and I-O Psychologists (LCIOP) Joint Task Force. (2017). The licensure issue in consulting and I-O psychology: A discussion paper. *Industrial and Organizational Psychology: Perspectives on Science and Practice, 10,* 144–181.

Locke, E. A. (2017). Say no to licensing: It is both impractical and immoral. *Industrial and Organizational Psychology: Perspectives on Science and Practice, 10,* 190–193.

Nagy, M. S., & Schroeder, D. A. (2019). Emerging issues in the licensure of I-O psychologists: Part I. *The Industrial and Organizational Psychologist, 56*(4). https://www.siop.org/Research-Publications/Items-of-Interest/ArtMID/19366/ArticleID/1876/Emerging-Issues-in-the-Licensure-of-I-O-Psychologists-Part-I

Shen, W. (2016). CSIOP members' views on licensure. *The Canadian Industrial & Organizational Psychologist, 33*(4), 1–3.

Shoenfelt, E. L. (2019a). I-O master's graduate survey. Survey conducted for E. L. Shoenfelt (Ed.) (2021). *Mastering the job market: Career issues for master's level industrial-organizational psychologist.* New York: Oxford University Press.

Shoenfelt, E. L. (2019b). I-O master's employer survey. Survey conducted for E. L. Shoenfelt (Ed.) (2021). *Mastering the job market: Career issues for master's level industrial-organizational psychologist.* New York: Oxford University Press.

Society for Industrial and Organizational Psychology, Inc. (n.d.a). *SIOP policy on licensure*. https://www.siop.org/Membership/Licensure-Policy-by-State

Society for Industrial and Organizational Psychology, Inc. (n.d.b). https://www.siop.org/About-SIOP/Mission

Society for Industrial and Organizational Psychology, Linc. (n.d.c). https://www.siop.org/Membership/Volunteering

Society for Industrial and Organizational Psychology, Inc. (2011). *SIOP 2011 membership survey: Licensed vs. not licensed report*. Bowling Green, OH: Author. /Licensed_vs_Not_Licensed_Report.pdf

Society for Industrial and Organizational Psychology, Inc. (2016). *Guidelines for education and training in industrial-organizational psychology*. Bowling Green, OH: Author. https://www.siop.org/Events-Education/Educators/Guidelines-Education-Training

Society for Industrial and Organizational Psychology, Inc. (2019). *SIOP Foundation 2017–2018 annual report*. https://www.siop.org/Portals/84/docs/foundation/Annual%20Reports/AR18.pdf?ver=2019-08-13-160156-720

Tett, R. P., Walser, B., Brown, C. Simonet, D. V., & Tonidandel, S. (2013). 2011 SIOP graduate program benchmarking survey part 3: Curriculum and competencies. *The Industrial-Organizational Psychologist, 50*(4), 69–89.

Tippins, N. T. (2006). Commentary from the field: An I-O psychologist's perspective on licensure. *APA Psychological Science Agenda*. https://www.apa.org/science/about/psa/2006/06/tippins

U.S. Department of Labor. (2019a). *Summary report for psychologists*. Washington, DC: Author. https://www.onetonline.org/link/summary/19-3031.02.

U.S. Department of Labor. (2019b). *Occupational outlook for psychologists*. Washington, DC: Author. https://www.bls.gov/ooh/life-physical-and-social-science/psychologists.htm.

Index

For the benefit of digital users, indexed terms that span two pages (e.g., 52–53) may, on occasion, appear on only one of those pages.

Tables and figures are indicated by *t* and *f* following the page number.